The GOD WHO SEES

BIBLE STUDY GUIDE | SIX SESSIONS

Kathie Lee Gifford
with Joanne Moody

Harper*Christian*
Resources

The God Who Sees Study Guide
© 2023 by Kathie Lee Gifford

Requests for information should be addressed to:
HarperChristian Resources, 3900 Sparks Dr. SE, Grand Rapids, Michigan 49546

ISBN 978-0-310-15680-2 (softcover)
ISBN 978-0-310-15681-9 (ebook)

First Printing July 2023 / Printed in the United States of America

23 24 25 26 27 LBC 5 4 3 2 1

Contents

A Note from Kathie Lee

Some years ago, I was staying at a friend's home. My friend had arranged for a "write," which is what those in the music industry call a songwriting session. On this day, I was scheduled to write with an amazing singer-songwriter named Nicole C. Mullen. I was familiar with her Grammy-nominated song, "I Know My Redeemer Lives," but I had never met her before.

As always, I prayed before our meeting that the Lord would lead us both and that we would be sensitive to what he wanted to accomplish in our lives and in our work. In Ephesians 3:20, Paul tells us that God will do "immeasurably more than all we ask or imagine." Even though I have memorized that scripture and prayed on it for years, it always surprises me when—like in this collaboration with Nicole—he actually does it! (Oh, me of little faith!)

I came to the session with something that I had been contemplating for several weeks: the biblical narrative of Hagar, who has one of the most heart-wrenching stories in the Old Testament. Hagar was the handmaiden of Sarah, Abraham's barren wife. She had been given (or sold) to Abraham by the Egyptian pharaoh. She was a slave with extremely limited personal freedom and therefore was considered of little value as a human being.

Abraham had been promised decades before that God would make him the father of nations—of so many people that they would be "as numerous as the stars in the sky" (Deuteronomy 28:62). This seemed impossible to them at the time, as Abraham and Sarah were already well into old age. Sarah, especially, had long since passed her childbearing years. She became increasingly frustrated as time passed and she finally did what so many us often do—she decided to take matters into her own hands. She literally threw Hagar into her husband's arms so that he and Hagar would bear a son whom Sarah could call her own and fulfill God's promise.

Hagar's story ended with calamitous results—as all stories do when we go outside of God's will. Yet the Lord used Sarah's terrible decision to bring about his greater purpose.

The song Nicole and I started writing that day was called "The God Who Sees," because that's the name Hagar attributed to the Almighty when he delivered her from the wilderness. But we were unable to finish the song because Nicole was leaving for a ministry trip to Africa and I had to return home to work on the *Today Show* the next day. I assured Nicole that I had the time to complete the song while she was gone, and we made a plan to get together again when we both returned.

What Nicole and I assumed we would end up with was a three-and-a-half-minute song for Danny Gokey to record. But instead the Holy Spirit inspired me to add the story of Ruth, another woman in despair living many centuries after Hagar. Then he prompted me to include the story of David hiding in the Judean wilderness from King Saul. Then I had the overwhelming feeling that I was to finish it with Mary of Magdala at the cross and at the tomb of Jesus.

I had become fascinated by how even though these individuals lived between 2,000 and 4,000 years ago, their stories felt as though they could have been ripped from today's headlines. Hagar was a slave who was sexually used and a single mother. Ruth was a widowed immigrant with seemingly no future. David was an anointed king but terrified and hiding in a cave. Mary of Magdala was mentally ill, having been tormented by seven demons.

But the same God—the God Who Sees—delivered them all from their despair. And this same God, who never changes, sees us in our despair and delivers us from it.

How to Use This Guide

The Bible tells the story of how Jesus, after a long day of teaching, got into a boat on the Sea of Galilee and instructed his disciples to journey to the other side. As the boat made its way across the lake, Jesus laid down on a cushion in the stern and fell asleep. Meanwhile, a furious storm arose, and the boat was nearly swamped with the waves. But Jesus didn't stir. Finally, the exasperated disciples cried out, "Teacher, don't you care if we drown?" (Mark 4:38).

It's a question that we often ask when we find ourselves in the storms of life. *Lord, don't you care if I drown?* We worry that God doesn't see the sky has grown dark. We are concerned that he doesn't see the waves have started rising. We are afraid that he doesn't see that we are being swamped by the squall. We wonder if he cares. But to all these fears and anxieties, the Lord says, "Quiet! Be still!" (verse 39). He has never taken his eye off us. He always knows what we are facing in this life . . . and he always has the power to deliver us.

In this study, we will look at the stories of five people in the Bible who all faced difficulties and came to the realization that they served the God Who Sees. Before you begin, keep in mind that there are a few ways you can go through this material. You can experience this study with others in a group (such as a Bible study, Sunday school class, or any other small-group gathering), or you may choose to go through the content on your own. Either way, know that the videos for each session are available for you to view at any time by following the instructions provided on the inside cover of this study guide.

Group Study

Each of the sessions is divided into two parts: (1) a group study section and (2) a personal study section. The group study section is intended to provide a basic framework on how to open your time together, get the most out of the video content, and discuss the key ideas together that were presented in the teaching. Each session includes the following:

- **Welcome:** A short note about the topic of the session for you to read on your own before you meet together as a group.

- **Connect:** A few icebreaker questions to get you and your group members thinking about the topic and interacting with each other.
- **Watch:** An outline of the key points that will be covered in each video teaching to help you follow along, stay engaged, and take notes.
- **Discuss:** Questions to help your group reflect on the material presented and apply it to your lives. In each session, you will be given four "suggested" questions and four "additional" questions to use as time allows.
- **Respond:** A short personal exercise to help reinforce the key ideas.
- **Pray:** A place for you to record prayer requests and praises for the week.

If you are doing this study in a group, make sure you have your own copy of this study guide so you can write down your thoughts, responses, and reflections and have access to the videos via streaming. You will also want to have a copy of *The God of the Way* book, as reading it alongside the curriculum will provide you with deeper insights. (See the notes at the beginning of each group session and personal study section on which chapters of the book you should read before the next group session.) Finally, keep these points in mind:

- **Facilitation:** If you are doing this study in a group, you will want to appoint someone to serve as a facilitator. This person will be responsible for starting the video and keeping track of time during discussions and activities. If *you* have been chosen for this role, there are some resources in the back of this guide that can help you lead your group through the study.

- **Faithfulness:** Your small group is a place where tremendous growth can happen as you reflect on the Bible, ask questions, and learn what God is doing in other people's lives. For this reason, be fully committed and attend each session so you can build trust and rapport with the other members.

- **Friendship:** The goal of any small group is to serve as a place where people can share, learn about God, and build friendships. So seek to make your group a safe place. Be honest about your thoughts and feelings . . . but also listen carefully to everyone else's thoughts, feelings, and opinions. Keep anything personal that your group members share in confidence so that you can create a community where people can heal, be challenged, and grow spiritually.

If you are going through this study on your own, read the opening Welcome section and reflect on the questions in the Connect section. Watch the video and use the prompts provided to take notes. Finally, personalize the questions and exercises in the Discuss and Respond sections. Close by recording any requests you want to pray about during the week.

Personal Study

As the name implies, the personal study is for you to work through on your own during the week. Each exercise is designed to help you explore the key ideas you uncovered during your group time and delve into passages of Scripture that will help you apply those principles to your life. Go at your own pace, doing a little each day or all at once, and spend a few moments in silence to listen to what God might be saying to you. Each personal study will include:

- **Opening:** A brief introduction to lead you into the personal study for the day.
- **Scripture:** A few passages on the topic of the day for you to read and review.
- **Reflection:** Questions for you to answer related to the passages you just read.
- **Prayer:** A prompt to help you express what you've studied in a prayer to God.

If you are doing this study as part of a group, and you are unable to finish (or even start) these personal studies for the week, you should still attend the group time. Be assured that you are still wanted and welcome even if you don't have your "homework" done. The group studies and personal studies are intended to help you hear what God wants you to hear and apply what he is saying to your life. So, as you go through this study, be listening for him to speak to you as you learn about what it means to trust in the *God Who Sees.*

Schedule

WEEK 1

BEFORE GROUP MEETING	Read the Introduction and Part 1 in *The God of the Way* Read the Welcome section (page 3)
GROUP MEETING	Discuss the Connect questions Watch the video teaching for session 1 Discuss the questions that follow as a group Do the closing exercise and pray (pages 3–14)
PERSONAL STUDY – DAY 1	Complete the daily study (pages 16–17)
PERSONAL STUDY – DAY 2	Complete the daily study (pages 18–19)
PERSONAL STUDY – DAY 3	Complete the daily study (pages 20–21)
PERSONAL STUDY – DAY 4	Complete the daily study (pages 22–23)
PERSONAL STUDY – DAY 5 (before week 2 group meeting)	Complete the daily study (pages 24–25) Read pages 126–134 in chapter 9 of *The God of the Way* Complete any unfinished personal studies

The Desert

GOD SEES US IN OUR STRUGGLES

The angel of the LORD found Hagar near a spring in the desert; it was the spring that is beside the road to Shur. And he said, "Hagar, slave of Sarai, where have you come from, and where are you going?" "I'm running away from my mistress Sarai," she answered. Then the angel of the LORD told her, "Go back to your mistress and submit to her." The angel added, "I will increase your descendants so much that they will be too numerous to count."

GENESIS 16:7–10

Deserts in Scripture

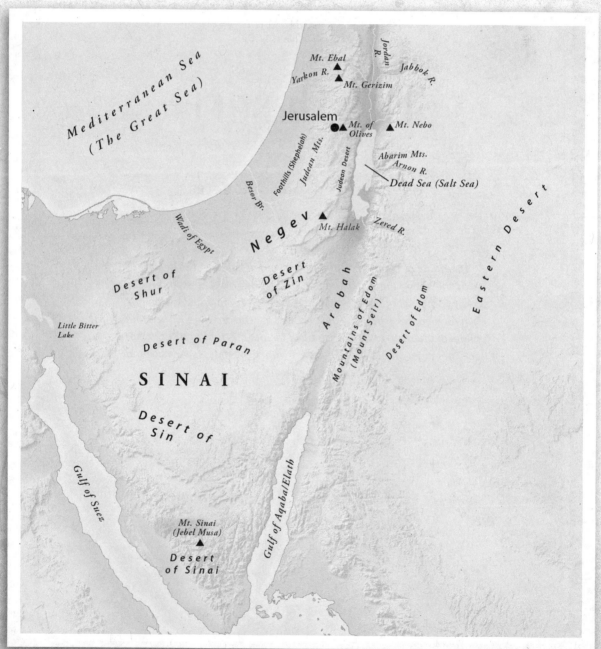

Mediterranean Sea
(The Great Sea)

Mt. Ebal
Yarkon R.
Mt. Gerizim
Jabbok R.
Jordan R.

Jerusalem
Mt. of Olives
Mt. Nebo

Abarim Mts.
Arnon R.
Dead Sea (Salt Sea)

Besor Br.
Foothills (Shephelah)
Judean Mts.
Judean Desert

Eastern Desert

N e g e v
Mt. Halak
Zered R.

Wadi of Egypt

Desert of Shur

Desert of Zin

Arabah

Mountains of Edom (Mount Seir)

Desert of Edom

Little Bitter Lake

Desert of Paran

SINAI

Desert of Sin

Gulf of Suez

Gulf of Aqaba/Elath

Mt. Sinai (Jebel Musa)

Desert of Sinai

Welcome | Read On Your Own

Welcome to *The God Who Sees*. Over the course of the next few weeks, you and your group will look at the stories of Hagar, Ruth, Boaz, David, and Mary of Magdala in the Bible and examine why they are so important today. But before we start out on that journey, we first need to take a look at *where* many of these events will take place: the desert.

When you hear the word *desert*, images of the Sahara, the Gobi, or the Mojave might spring to mind. You may picture an arid place of desolation and cracked earth. The deserts in Israel—which cover a full two-thirds of the country's landmass—at first glance seem to fit this description. But there is life in those deserts! There are streams of water that are hidden. There is plant life that you don't expect to see. There are birds receiving sustenance from some source. What's more, these deserts serve as key geographical locations in Scripture. Abraham, Jacob, Moses, Elijah, and John the Baptist—to name just a few—all spent significant amounts of time in the desert. It was there, in those dry, difficult, and seemingly desolate places, that many of them encountered God. It was in the deserts where many of their lives were transformed and they received a new mission from the Lord.

You probably have not spent a lot of time in physical deserts like these characters. But you have certainly witnessed your share of desert experiences. Times of spiritual dryness, struggle, fear, anxiety, loneliness, doubt, and even depression. Times in your life that you would rather forget. But also times when you most depended on God to get you through this life and most clearly heard his still, small voice speak into your life.

The desert can surprise you. The desert can change you. The desert can transform you. The desert is where God will meet with his people—including you.

Connect | 15 minutes

If any of your group members don't know each other, take a few minutes to introduce yourselves. Then, to get things started, discuss one of the following questions:

- How would you describe your primary goal or hope for participating in this study? (In other words, why are you here?)

  — *or* —

- What are some "desert" or "wilderness" seasons that you have gone through in your life? What did you learn from those experiences?

Watch | 20 minutes

Now it's time to watch the video for this session, which you can access by playing the DVD or through streaming (see the instructions provided on the inside front cover). As you watch, use the following outline to record any thoughts or concepts that stand out to you.

I. What is unique about the deserts and wilderness areas in Israel?

   A. The Judean desert is close to the city of Jerusalem (about thirteen miles away).

   1. You can't read the Bible without running into the words *desert* or *wilderness* almost all the time. (The words occur nearly 300 times in Scripture.[1])

   2. The topography of Israel is varied and beautiful. Galilee, in the north, is an agricultural area. There are palm trees in Jericho. A mile away, you are at the Dead Sea.

   3. When you look at stories in the Bible, you might expect people had to walk for miles to get to the desert. But the deserts were in close proximity to the cities and villages.

   B. The wilderness areas in Israel look barren at first glance, but there is life in the desert.

   1. There are streams of water that are hidden. There is plant life there in the desert that you don't expect to see. There are birds that are getting sustenance from somewhere!

The Deserts of Israel

The nation of Israel is comprised of an area about 290 miles north-to-south and 85 miles east-to-west. Yet in spite of the country's small size, it has several diverse geographic regions, ranging from lush greenery in the northern Galilee region, to snows on Mount Hermon in the northeast, to sandy beaches in the western coastal region. But the largest geographic region in Israel—comprising more than half the country—is made up of four primary deserts.

The Arabah Desert. The Arabah is located in a valley that begins near the Dead Sea and stretches south to the city of Eilat on the Gulf of Aqaba. The climate of the Arabah is harsh, with an annual rainfall of only a few inches and temperatures in the summer that soar to more than 113 degrees Fahrenheit during summer. The Arabah is mentioned in Deuteronomy 4:49 as part of the territory the Israelites took from the Amorite kings east of the Jordan River.

The Negev. The Negev is the largest desert in Israel. It is located in the southern portion of the country and is characterized by rocky mountains, craters, and dry river (wadis). The northern portion of the region receives around 12 inches of rainfall annually, with fertile soil in places suitable for agriculture, while the western region only receives around 10 inches and has sandy soil. The Negev was the home of Abraham for some time (see Genesis 13:1) and was the route that Moses instructed the twelve spies to take to explore Canaan (see Numbers 13:17).

The Zin Desert. The Zin Desert (also known as the Wilderness of Zin) is located between the Arabah and the Negev. In modern times, it is most famous for being the expedition site of British explorer Thomas Lawrence, better known as Lawrence of Arabia. In biblical times, the Zin was the location where God performed the miracle of bringing water from a rock during the Israelites' exodus from Egypt (see Numbers 27:14).[2]

The Judean Desert. The Judean desert lies east of Jerusalem and stretches from the north of Jericho to the southern end of the Dead Sea. It is the location of Ein Gedi, an oasis where David hid from King Saul (see 1 Samuel 23:29); Masada, where King Herod the Great built a fortress on a rock plateau; and Qumran, where an early Christian group known as the Essenes hid a number of writings (called the Dead Sea Scrolls) that were discovered in 1947.[3]

2. There are crevices in the hills of Israel where streams are suddenly created during the rainy season. These dry riverbeds, known as *wadis* (Hebrew *nahal*), can be dangerous when the storms come. If you're in a *wadi* when that happens . . . you're a deadie.

3. What we need to know as backstory to the deserts and wildernesses that we read about in Scripture is that they were dry and arid but they also had good routes for people to go through them.

C. The characters we read about in the Bible generally didn't go into the deserts unless they were running from law (hiding out) or seeking solace with God.

1. David hid in the desert when he was on the run from King Saul (see 1 Samuel 23:14).

2. John the Baptist sought solace with God in the wilderness and spent most of his life there. He was the "voice of one calling in the wilderness" (Matthew 3:3) who prepared the way for the coming of Jesus, the promised Messiah.

3. There was a fantastic explosion around AD 6 of people looking for God in the wilderness. More than sixty-five monasteries were built out in the middle of nowhere.

II. What is the spiritual significance of the deserts that we read about in the Bible?

A. The deserts in Israel seem void of human life, but we know from stories in the Bible that people survived there. It's also depicted in Scripture as a spiritual place of exile.

1. Given this, it is interesting that the people whom God spoke to in the desert became great leaders. We see this in the story of Moses and the Israelites wandering around in the wilderness for forty years. God used that time to speak to his people.

2. Moses told the people, "The LORD your God has blessed you in all that you have done; He has known your wanderings through this great wilderness. These forty years the LORD your God has been with you; you have not lacked anything" (Deuteronomy 2:7 NASB).

3. Just as there are hidden streams that support life in the desert, there are things hidden in our hearts that God unearths during desert seasons. God was using the Israelites' time in the desert to captivate their attention. All the distractions were taken away.

B. When we are in a desert season, we can be assured God is with us in the midst of it all.

1. God speaks to us during the worst times in our lives—what we call our "wilderness journeys." In every story in the Bible where people were exiled, were in a wilderness, or were in a desert, there were miracles that took place.

2. God is a God of miracles. He has not forgotten us in the desert season we might be living through right now. He will never leave us or forsake us (see Deuteronomy 31:6).

3. God is *El Elyon*, "from everlasting to everlasting." Our covenant in Yeshua, through whom all good things come, will never been broken because of our circumstances.

III. What do we learn from the story of Hagar's experience in the desert?

   A. Hagar is an interesting character in the Bible because her story is so complex. Her name means "forsaken," but it can also mean "to flee."

   1. Names have great meaning in Scripture, but it doesn't mean the person had to forever carry the history of the name. As we will see as we study the story of Hagar, even though she fled from Sarah, the Lord never left her or abandoned her.

   2. Not much of Hagar's backstory is given in the Old Testament except a mention that she was an Egyptian slave given to Sarah (see Genesis 16:1). Her story is tragic at first.

   3. God had promised Abraham and Sarah that they would become the parents of a great nation. But Sarah got tired of waiting. So she literally pushed Hagar into her husband's arms and said to him, "Go, sleep with my slave; perhaps I can build a family through her" (Genesis 16:2).

   4. Immediately after Hagar became pregnant, Sarah complained to Abraham. He responded, "Your slave is in your hands" (Genesis 16:6). In other words, "She's your problem." He did not come to the rescue of the woman that he had impregnated.

The Desert Fathers

The Byzantine Era—especially during the fourth to seventh centuries—saw an explosion of Christian ascetics moving out of the cities to find solace with God in the desert. But as far back as the late second century, a group of Christians in Egypt (known as the "Desert Fathers") had paved the way by moving out of the pagan cities to lead a solitary life devoted to God in the Sahara Desert. Here are a few of these individuals who are remembered by history.

Anthony of Egypt (c. 251–356) was a wealthy man who heard a sermon in which Jesus said, "If you want to be perfect, go, sell your possessions and give to the poor, and you will have treasure in heaven" (Matthew 19:21). Anthony took these words to heart, and sometime around AD 270, he exchanged his worldly possessions for a small hut in the desert. Over time, his model attracted other like-minded Christians who desired to separate themselves from the world and establish communities in the desert dedicated to following after God.[4]

Pachomius (c. 292–348) of Thebes was imprisoned by the Romans at the age of twenty and witnessed the kindness of Christians who brought him food and provisions each day. He became a Christ-follower when he was released and moved into the desert. Once there, he built small houses where people could live together in Christian communities. At his death in AD 348, more than 3,000 of his monasteries dotted the Egyptian desert.[5]

Macarius the Egyptian (c. 300–391) moved to the desert at the age of thirty and remained there for the rest of his life. He was known and greatly sought after for his unusual judgment and discernment, earning him the nickname *Paidarion Geron*, "the young man with the elders' wisdom." Around 374, he was banished to an island in the Nile for his opposition to a doctrine known as Arianism, but he was released shortly thereafter.[6]

Arsenius of Rome (c. 354–455) served in the court of Theodosius I in Constantinople. He was surrounded by wealth in this role but increasingly felt the need to renounce the ways of the world. After eleven years of service, he traveled by ship to Alexandria and joined a Christian community in the desert. A quiet and often silent man, he is noted for the adage, "Many times have I repented of having spoken, but never have I repented of having remained silent."[7]

B. Hagar and her son, Ishmael, were cast out of Abraham and Sarah's family when Isaac was born to them. We then read, "When the water in the skin was gone, [Hagar] put the boy under one of the bushes" (Genesis 21:15).

    1. Hagar put Ishmael under a bush and walked away so she didn't have to witness him dying (see Genesis 21:16). We can only imagine her desperation in this environment.

    2. But then we read, "God heard the boy crying" (Genesis 21:17). God *saw* Hagar in the desert. He came to her and provided water for her and her son.

    3. God provided for Hagar and Ishmael's physical needs and again promised to make Ishmael into a great nation (see Genesis 21:18). No matter what happens, we can trust that God sees us in the middle of the most desperate time of our lives. He *does* see.

IV. What is significant about the name that Hagar gives to God?

    A. It is interesting to note that Hagar, a female Egyptian slave, was the one who got to name God. There is no hierarchy with God. He says everyone is a priceless treasure.

    B. When we talk about Hagar and the promises that God made to her concerning Ishmael, there is an important theme about intimacy with God in a desert that we should not miss.

        1. The Hebrew word for *desert* is *midbar*. There are no vowels in the Hebrew language, so the name is written MDBR. Hagar named God "the God who sees me." But she named her son Ishmael, which means "the one who hears God" or "God hears him." God sees and hears.

2. The word *medaber* in Hebrew, spelled the same way (*MDBR*), means "to speak." So, the same word for *desert* in Hebrew is the same word for *speak*. No matter what we are going through in life, God is speaking to us in the desert. It's the same word!

C. Hagar's experience in the desert has several applications for our lives.

1. Paul tells us that we "are being transformed into [God's] image with ever-increasing *glory*" (2 Corinthians 3:18). We are going from glory to glory, from strength to strength, but there will still be some wilderness seasons in the meantime.

2. We have to trust that God sees us in our desert (*midbar*) and speaks to us in the midst of it (*medaber*). When we are suffering, we focus on ourselves, but what we should do in the midst of a valley is trust God and worship him (see Job 13:15).

3. The story of Hagar and Ishmael reveals that God's promises are for a thousand generations (see Deuteronomy 7:9). All God's promises in him are *yes* and *amen* (see 2 Corinthians 1:20). We have to choose in our desert experiences to serve the Lord.

Discuss | 35 minutes

Take some time to discuss what you just watched by answering the following questions. There are some suggested questions below to help you begin your discussion, but feel free to pick any of the additional questions as time allows.

Suggested Questions

1. In the Bible, deserts represent a number of different things that are negative in nature, such as the punishment awaiting rebels (see Psalm 68:7), neglectful leadership (see Jeremiah 12:10–11), and a warning of divine punishment (see Isaiah 32:11–16).[8] But what are some of the positive things that deserts represent in Scripture?

2. Read Exodus 3:1–6. Moses had fled to Midian after killing an Egyptian who was beating a Hebrew. It was there, in a wilderness near Mount Horeb, that Moses had this encounter with God. What did the Lord say about the ground on which Moses was standing? Why do you think God chose to appear to Moses in the desert?

3. The name that Hagar gave to God was *El Roi*, "the God who sees me." She gave her son the name *Ishmael*, which means "the one who hears" or "God hears him." Based on what you know of Hagar's story, what is the significance of these names? What do they imply that Hagar had recognized about the God of Abraham?

4. Hagar went through a literal "desert experience" when she was forced to leave Abraham's family and fend for herself in the desert of Beersheba. But we often find ourselves in our own desert experiences—difficult seasons in which we wonder if God

sees us and cares about our situation. What does the story of Hagar reveal about how God meets us in those times? What encouragement do you glean from her story?

Additional Questions

5. Read 1 Samuel 23:14. People in biblical times may have passed *through* the deserts, but none of them *remained* in the deserts unless they were running from the law or seeking solace with God. What was the situation that led to David spending a lot of time in the desert? What does this verse imply about God's presence with David in the desert?

6. What does this passage imply about the reasons why John the Baptist might have chosen to spend extended periods of time in the desert?

7. Peter summed up the life of a believer in this way: "In all this you greatly rejoice, though now for a little while you may have had to suffer grief in all kinds of trials" (1 Peter 1:6). What do you think Peter meant when he said that we will have to suffer grief "for a little while"? What is the promise for all believers in Jesus who endure trials in this life?

8. When we are in a desert season, we have the choice to focus on ourselves and our suffering or focus on God and his promises. What are some of the things that help you to keep your focus on the Lord when you are going through a desert experience?

Respond | 10 minutes

Review the outline for the video teaching and any notes you took. In the space below, write down your most significant takeaway from this session.

Pray | 10 minutes

Praying for one another is one of the most important things you can do as a community. So use this time wisely and make it more than just a "closing prayer" to end your group experience. Be intentional about sharing your prayers, reviewing how God is answering your prayers, and actually praying for one another as a group. Use the space below to write down any requests so that you and your group members can continue to pray about them in the week ahead.

Name	Request

Personal Study

You are on a journey toward a better understanding of the God Who Sees. A key part of that growth, regardless of where you are spiritually, involves studying Scripture. This is the goal of these personal studies—to help you explore what the Bible has to say and apply the Word of God to your life. As you work through each of these exercises, be sure to write down your responses to the questions, as you will be given a few minutes to share your insights at the start of the next session if you are doing this study with others. If you are reading *The God of the Way* alongside this study, first read pages 121–126 in chapter 9 of the book.

- Day 1 -

God Speaks in the Wilderness

The Judean wilderness is not exactly prime real estate. The terrain is rough, barren, and unaccommodating. It's a place where people in the Bible (and in history) went to hide, knowing that no one would likely follow them there. The desert contrasts with humanity's first home: the garden of Eden. The Bible states that the garden was lush with life. A river ran through it. Fruit trees blossomed. Most importantly, the Lord was present there (see Genesis 2).

It's tempting to look at a place like the Judean desert and assume that God *isn't* there. Why would he be? The land is sparse and dry. But again and again in the pages of the Bible, we see God choosing to meet his people in this desolate landscape. The desert is the place where God first spoke to Abraham, promising to make his lineage into a great nation (Genesis 12:1–3). It is where he comforted Jacob and promised to be with him wherever he went (see 28:13–15). It is where he spoke to John the Baptist (see Mark 1:3). It is also where Jesus encountered the power of God's Word before beginning his public ministry (see Matthew 4:1–11).

The desert, both back then and today, is a place where God speaks to his people. As you discussed in this week's group time, the Hebrew word translated as "wilderness" is *midbar*. There are no vowels in the Hebrew language, so the word is spelled *MDBR*. The Hebrew word translated "to speak" is *medaber*, which is also written *MDBR* in Hebrew. In the wilderness . . . God speaks.

What word describes your wilderness experience? Burned out? Depressed? Hopeless? Spiritually dry? Emotionally depleted? You don't have to be thriving in your ministry, family, or community to hear from God. In fact, it's often in the quiet—when you've hit rock bottom and nothing is going well in your life—that you are most primed to hear God's voice. When you've come to the end of yourself in the desert place is often when God begins something brand new.

Read | Deuteronomy 32:10–14

Reflect

1. The Lord had denied the Israelites entry into the promised land after they had rebelled against him at Kadesh Barnea and doubted that he would give the land to them. As a consequence, they were forced to wander in the wilderness for forty years. How is the desert described in this passage? What did God do for the people there?

2. Notice the vivid descriptions that are given in verses 13–14. How do these depictions of Israel's time in the wilderness contrast with how you think about life and fruitfulness in the desert?

3. Think about the last time you found yourself in a wilderness season. What led you there? How did it feel—or does it feel—to be in that type of spiritual landscape?

4. Again and again in the Bible we read how God met his people in the midst of their wilderness experience. Has God ever met *you* in the wilderness? If so, how did he make his presence known to you in that season of your life?

Pray | Put yourself into the Deuteronomy passage. Replace the mentions of Israel (*him*) with *me*. Write (or read) the passage in this way. Reflect on how it feels to be cared for by God just as he cared for his people in the wilderness.

– Day 2 –

Tested in the Wilderness

There are many people in the Bible who found themselves in the desert or wilderness. But chief among them is Jesus. Scripture tells us that the Holy Spirit led Jesus into the wilderness "to be tempted," or tested, by the devil (Matthew 4:1). Commentators point out that Jesus' time in the wilderness (forty days) parallels the time that the Israelites spent in the desert (forty years) as they were tested by God.[9] Unlike the Israelites, however, Jesus passed his test on the first try.

Even though Jesus was tempted in the wilderness by Satan, he never wavered. He recalled Scripture, declared it aloud to the evil one, and resisted the temptation to abandon his call from the Father—all after forty days and nights of *fasting*. His time in the wilderness immediately followed his baptism, where the Spirit of the Lord descended on him (see Matthew 3:16) and a voice was heard from heavean that said, "This is my Son, whom I love; with him I am well pleased" (verse 17), and it immediately preceded his public ministry. The desert was a place of preparation for Jesus—a place of testing to ensure that he was ready for what was to come.

The desert serves many purposes in Scripture and in our lives. Sometimes we find ourselves in that barren place due to exhaustion, depression, and burnout. But sometimes we find ourselves there in preparation for what is next. Often, it's both. The dark and dry seasons prepare us for what is to come and makes us stronger.

Jesus showed incredible strength in the desert. But we may not show as much strength, especially if we've been fasting for forty days and forty nights. We are anxious in the desert. We grumble and complain. *How long do we have to be here?* But we're not expected to manage our desert times perfectly or even to pass whatever test in which we find ourselves. Jesus is the author and perfecter of our faith (see Hebrews 12:2).

Just as he drew strength from the Word of God during his time in the desert, so we can draw our strength from him, the Word of Life.

Read | Matthew 4:1–11 and Luke 4:1–13

Reflect

1. Each of these passages records three specific ways that Satan tested Jesus in the wilderness. What was the nature of those temptations? What did the devil want Jesus to do? Why do you think Jesus was tempted in this way in preparation for ministry?

2. What is the significance of the enemy tempting Jesus while he was in a period of fasting? What does this tell us about the times when the enemy will tempt us?

3. How did Jesus respond to each temptation that Satan lobbed at him? What does this reveal about the way in which we should battle temptation?

4. What wilderness time in your life prepared you for something else? What were you being prepared for? Why was this time in the desert necessary for that preparation?

Pray | End your time in prayer. If you are in a wilderness season, ask God to help you understand what he is preparing you to do. Ask Jesus to bring you comfort, peace, and knowledge from the Word that will get you through this time and strengthen your faith.

-Day 3-

The God Who *Always* Sees

"Hey, Mom, look at me do this!" "Hey, Dad, watch me do this!" Every parent has heard his or her child exclaim something like this as that child did a somersault on the trampoline or tossed a ball in the air and caught it. Children need their parents' attention. It is crucial to their development. If we are honest with ourselves, this doesn't change much as we grow older.

We long to be seen. Not for doing somersaults or throwing balls in the air but to be seen for who we are as individuals. Often, the truth is that we *don't* get this kind of recognition from others. We are *not* seen and known. But even if this is our reality, we can be confident that we have a God who always sees us, knows us, and loves us for who we are.

This is what Hagar—status-less, penniless, and hopeless—discovered about God during her time in the desert. She first found herself in the wilderness after fleeing from her mistress, Sarah, who was mistreating her. To make matters worse, Hagar was carrying Abraham's child. Pregnant, alone, and afraid, she felt the *opposite* of seen. As a slave, she had no rights. She was invisible in her culture. She was voiceless and faceless to all but one: *God*.

While in the desert, Hagar was visited by the angel of the Lord who made a great promise to her: "I will increase your descendants so much that they will be too numerous to count" (Genesis 16:10). The Lord's words caused Hagar to respond, "You are the God who sees me" (verse 13). She called him *El Roi*—the God Who Sees.

How good it is to feel seen and be known. In Hagar's story, it is a promise to us. The Lord sees us according to his prophetic promises over our lives: as his children (see 1 John 3:1), as the righteousness of Christ (see 2 Corinthians 5:21), as made according to his image (see Genesis 1:26–27), as brand-new creations in Jesus (see 2 Corinthians 5:17), and as living temples for his Holy Spirit (see 1 Corinthians 3:16). He made us his disciple makers (see Matthew 28:19), his light in the darkness, and his ambassadors of hope and faith in this dark world (see Matthew 5:13–16).

Read | Genesis 16:7–14

Reflect

1. The Bible doesn't reveal exactly what Hagar did to "despise her mistress" (verse 4) or what Sarah then did when she "mistreated Hagar" (verse 6). But the situation was so tense that it caused Hagar to see fleeing into the desert as her best option. It was there that the angel of the Lord (God) found her near a spring. How did the angel of the Lord address Hagar in verse 8? What does this say about Hagar's status?

2. The Lord told Hagar, "Go back to your mistress and submit to her" (verse 9), which could not have been an easy instruction for Hagar to follow given the circumstances. But what promise did God then make to her? How did he reassure her in verse 11?

3. As we have seen, this episode caused Hagar to declare that the Lord was "the God who sees" (verse 13). Who in your life really sees and knows you? How does it feel to be around this person or around this group of people in your life?

4. Do you feel seen by God? How do you need to be seen by God today?

Pray | Believe that God sees you today. He sees your misery. He sees your joy. He sees the good in you and the bad. Spend a few moments in silence, allowing God to see you for who you are, trusting that he loves you and accepts you.

-Day 4-

God Keeps His Promises

When it comes to desert seasons, what happens in the desert does not stay in the desert. God does not just intervene when we find ourselves in the midst of a wilderness and leave us once we are out of it. Whatever he tells us in the desert times of our lives will remain true for the rest of our lives. Whatever promises he made, he will keep. We see this in the promise that God made to Hagar about her son, Ishmael.

We don't talk much about Ishmael. After all, Isaac was the son of God's promise to Abraham and Sarah. We see Ishmael as the offspring of a bad plan concocted by Sarah to intervene in God's plan. Ishmael is often passed over in our minds and his legacy forgotten. But God did not forget Ishmael, nor the promise he made when Ishmael was in Hagar's womb. As he said to Hagar during her first trip to the desert, "I will increase your descendants so much that they will be too numerous to count" (Genesis 16:10).

Ishmael was the firstborn son of Abraham. But when he was thirteen, Sarah gave birth to Isaac and then told her husband, "Get rid of that slave woman and her son, for that woman's son will never share in the inheritance with my son Isaac" (21:10). We know the decision to send Hagar and Ishmael into the desert "distressed Abraham greatly" (verse 11). He had to believe God's promise that he would not only save Ishmael's life but also make "the son of the slave into a nation also, because he is your offspring" (verse 13).

Once in the desert, Hagar was convinced her son would die of thirst or starvation. But God kept his promises. The angel of the Lord visited her again and said, "What is the matter, Hagar? Do not be afraid; God has heard the boy crying as he lies there. Lift the boy up and take him by the hand, for I will make him into a great nation" (verses 17–18). God personally reassured Hagar on *two occasions* that he saw her and had plans for her and her son.

You need look no further than Scripture to know that God made good on this promise. Ishmael did survive the desert and had many descendants. God does not forget what he tells us in the desert. His word, even in desolate landscapes, does not return void.

Read | Genesis 25:7–18 and Isaiah 55:9–11

Reflect

1. Abraham lived for many years on this earth and then "breathed his last and died at a good old age" (Genesis 25:8). Both of his sons—Isaac and Ishmael—reunited at least on this occasion and buried him in a cave (see verse 9). According to the account of Ishmael's descendants in verses 12–18, what kind of lineage did he leave behind?

2. The prophet Isaiah wrote that God's ways are higher than our ways. In other words, we can't always comprehend what God is doing or how he will deliver on his promises . . . but we can trust that he always will. What metaphors are used to describe God's word in this passage? What does this say about the nature of God's promises to us?

3. When is a time that you saw this to be true—that God made good on his word in spite of your doubts or your sense that any kind of resolution to the situation was impossible?

4. What promises are you still waiting on God to deliver in your life? How does it feel to wait? How can Ishmael's story give you hope as you wait?

Pray | Think about a promise God made to you. If you've seen it fulfilled, thank him for it. If you're still waiting on it, ask him to be with you as you do. If you're able, write down any promises you can think of that God has fulfilled for you or for others you know. Use these as encouragement that the promise you're waiting on will also be fulfilled.

-Day 5-

Worshiping in the Desert

When we are in the desert, what is it we think about? *The desert*. We think about our depression, anxiety, and fears. We focus on our trials, struggles, and challenges. We think about the desolation and wilderness we see around us because it is all we can see. When Hagar found herself in a desert for the second time, in a barren landscape with no water, her focus was on her life-threatening plight and the seemingly hopeless situation for herself and her son. But God changed Hagar's focus. The Bible says that he "opened her eyes" and showed her a well just off in the distance filled with life-saving water.

This is what worship does for us in the desert. It opens our eyes to something greater than the desolation before us. It reminds us of who God is and that he is near. It takes our focus off ourselves so we can drink from the well of living water. Of course, worshiping in the desert is not our natural inclination. It requires effort to shift our focus. But when we do, we provide space for God to move. We allow our imaginations to explore the possibility that things could get better. We start to believe we are *not* doomed to die in the desert.

As you have learned this week, the desert is anything but desolate. It is the place where God often chooses to meet with us, speak to us, and begin something new in us. Even if you don't know why you are in the desert—even if you are not seeing any growth or don't sense that you are hearing God's voice—worship still serves as a reminder that something is happening beneath the surface. God is at work in your desert. Worship might be just what your heart needs to stay attuned to his voice.

Read | Habakkuk 3:17–19

Reflect

1. Habakkuk was a prophet in the Old Testament who was active sometime around 607 BC, during the reign of King Jehoiakim of Judah.[10] In his book, he asks why God would allow the nation to grow evil under the leadership of this king and why he would allow

the Babylonians to conquer Judah. For much of the book, Habakkuk laments the fate of his people, but by chapter 3, he remembers who God is and begins to worship. How does Habakkuk describe the landscape around him? How does he describe God?

2. What does Habakkuk compare himself to in this passage? What does this tell us about how worship affects him?

3. Think about the last time you truly worshiped God. This could be at your church, in your home, or anywhere you felt connected to God. How did this time in worship impact you? How did it make you feel about whatever you were facing at the time?

4. In your current season, what are some things (if any) that keep you from worshiping God? How could you worship God today, even if you are in the wilderness?

Pray | Spend time today just worshiping God. Thank him for what he has done. Name his attributes: good, kind, strong, Father. If you're able, assume a posture of worship by kneeling, or raising your hands, or whatever helps you feel less distracted and able to worship him.

For Next Week

Before you meet again with your group, read pages 126–134 in chapter 9 of *The God of the Way*. Also go back and complete any of the study and reflection questions from this personal study that you weren't able to finish.

WEEK 2

BEFORE GROUP MEETING	Read pages 126–134 in chapter 9 of *The God of the Way* Read the Welcome section (page 29)
GROUP MEETING	Discuss the Connect questions Watch the video teaching for session 2 Discuss the questions that follow as a group Do the closing exercise and pray (pages 29–40)
PERSONAL STUDY – DAY 1	Complete the daily study (pages 42–43)
PERSONAL STUDY – DAY 2	Complete the daily study (pages 44–45)
PERSONAL STUDY – DAY 3	Complete the daily study (pages 46–47)
PERSONAL STUDY – DAY 4	Complete the daily study (pages 48–49)
PERSONAL STUDY – DAY 5 (before week 3 group meeting)	Complete the daily study (pages 50–51) Read pages 135–144 in chapter 10 of *The God of the Way* Complete any unfinished personal studies

Hagar

GOD COMFORTS US IN OUR TRIALS

[Hagar] went off and sat down about a bowshot away, for she thought, "I cannot watch the boy die." And as she sat there, she began to sob. God heard the boy crying, and the angel of God called to Hagar from heaven and said to her, "What is the matter, Hagar? Do not be afraid; God has heard the boy crying as he lies there. Lift the boy up and take him by the hand, for I will make him into a great nation."

GENESIS 21:16–18

Israel in Hagar's Day

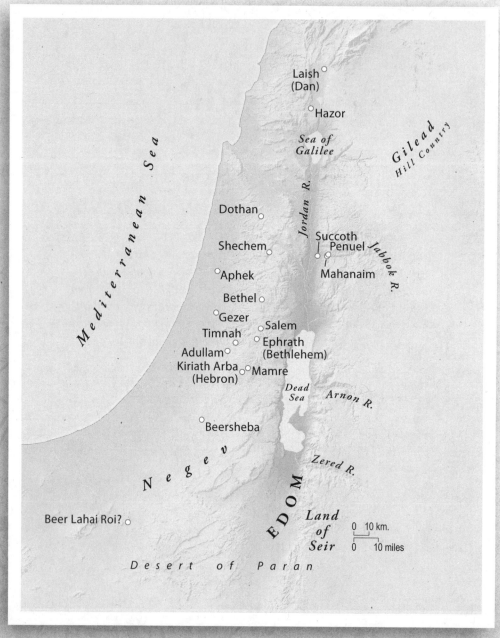

Laish (Dan)

Hazor

Sea of Galilee

Gilead Hill Country

Mediterranean Sea

Dothan

Shechem

Aphek

Bethel

Gezer

Timnah

Salem

Adullam

Ephrath (Bethlehem)

Kiriath Arba (Hebron)

Mamre

Jordan R.

Succoth
Penuel

Jabbok R.

Mahanaim

Dead Sea

Arnon R.

Beersheba

Negev

Zered R.

EDOM

Land of Seir

Beer Lahai Roi?

Desert of Paran

0   10 km.

0   10 miles

Welcome | Read On Your Own

In the last session, you looked at some of the features of the deserts in Israel, learned about what deserts represent in Scripture, and saw that God often chose these barren places to meet with his followers and transform their lives. One such person whom God met in the wilderness—on two separate occasions—was a woman named Hagar. She was the first person to give God a name, calling him El Roi, "the God who sees me" (Genesis 16:13).

What is interesting about Hagar is that she was an Egyptian slave. As such, she had two major strikes against her: (1) she was in the lowest social order, and (2) she was a foreigner and outsider living in Israelite society. She must have felt unseen by everyone. But it was when Hagar was at her lowest points in life, trying to survive out in the desert, that God made it abundantly clear that he not only saw her but also cared about her.

Perhaps you can relate to Hagar's story. Maybe at times you have felt like just one of the billions of people on this planet, unseen and unknown by others, and especially by God. You've wondered how God could possibly know your struggles and what you are facing in the mass of all the other people on this planet. But as you dig deeper into Hagar's story in this session, you will learn the truth about how God feels about you. The Lord did not see her as a foreigner, or as an outcast, or as a person whose only worth in society was determined by what she could produce for another person. No, God *saw* her and *valued* her.

So as you go through this session, let Hagar's story give you hope. It is during the rock-bottom moments in life that God reaches out to you. He reminds you that he is always there. In fact, he never left you in the first place.

Connect | 15 minutes

Welcome to session 2 of *The God Who Sees*. To get things started for this group time, discuss one of the following questions:

- What is a key insight or takeaway from last week's personal study that you would like to share with the group?

— *or* —

- When is a time in your life that God revealed his strength to you when you were at your weakest? What did you learn about God through that situation?

Watch | 20 minutes

Now watch the video for this session (remember that you can access this video via streaming by following the instructions printed on the inside front cover). As you watch, use the following outline to record any thoughts or concepts that stand out to you.

I. What are some of highlights—or *low*lights—of Hagar's story in the book of Genesis?

   A. Hagar was an Egyptian slave who was in service to Sarah as her maid (see Genesis 16:1). Hagar's name means "forsaken" and also means "to flee."

      1. God had promised children to Sarah and Abraham, but nothing was happening. So Sarah pushed Hagar into the arms of her husband (see Genesis 16:2–3).

      2. When Hagar knew she was pregnant, "she began to despise her mistress" (Genesis 16:4). Sarah said to Abraham, "You are responsible for the wrong I am suffering" (verse 5).

      3. Sarah continued, "I put my slave in your arms, and now that she knows she is pregnant, she despises me. May the LORD judge between you and me" (Genesis 16:5).

   B. Abraham responded to Sarah, "Your slave is in your hands" (Genesis 16:6).

      1. Abraham basically dismissed what was happening. He told Sarah to "do with her whatever you think best" (Genesis 16:6). Sarah responded by mistreating Hagar.

      2. Hagar lived up to her name and fled. In her day—in the patriarchal culture in which she lived—she was the bottom of the bottom, a pariah, and had no rights.

Hagar in Jewish Tradition

The biblical story of Hagar, as told in Genesis, contains few details about her life. Hagar is described as an Egyptian slave who, at the direction of Sarah, became a concubine to her husband, Abraham. When Hagar became pregnant, she then "began to despise her mistress" (Genesis 16:4), which led to Sarah mistreating her to the point that she fled into the desert. There she was met by the Lord, who instructed her to return to Sarah, which she did. But after the birth of Isaac, she and her son, Ishmael, were permanently cast out of the family.

This is all we learn about Hagar in Scripture. However, the *Midrash*—an ancient Jewish commentary on the Hebrew Scriptures—contains additional stories about her life. According to one source, Hagar was the daughter of the Egyptian pharaoh. The Bible relates that when Abraham and Sarah traveled to Egypt to escape a famine, Pharaoh saw that Sarah was beautiful and took her into his palace. This led to the Lord inflicting serious diseases on Pharaoh's household because, unknown to him, she was Abraham's wife (see Genesis 12:10–20). When God revealed this to Pharaoh, he instructed Abraham and Sarah to leave.

But the *Midrash* states that before the couple left, Pharaoh said, "It is better for Hagar to be a slave in Sarah's house than mistress in her own," and gave his daughter to serve Sarah. In this sense, Hagar's name is interpreted as *Ha-Agar*, or "this is reward." Hagar is later held up in some accounts in the *Midrash* as an example of godliness, for unlike others who feared they would die if they saw an angel of the Lord (see Judges 13:9–22), she was not frightened when the angel appeared and actually conversed with the Lord (see Genesis 16:7–10).

Other narratives about Hagar's life take a less favorable view of her character. In one account, the rabbis state that when Hagar despised her mistress (see Genesis 16:4), she gossiped about Sarah, saying, "She is certainly not as godly as she pretends to be, for in all the years of her married life she has had no children, while I conceived at once." Later, when Hagar "went on her way" (Genesis 21:14) into the Desert of Beersheba, the rabbis infer that this meant Hagar slipped back into idolatry. The fact that Hagar then selected an Egyptian wife for Ishmael (see Genesis 21:21) is seen as further evidence supporting this point.[11]

3. Hagar could not "pick herself up by the bootstraps" or do anything to improve her situation because society would not allow her to do anything.

C. The story is not a shining moment for Abraham and Sarah—and it becomes not a shining moment for the pregnant Hagar when she runs away. She would have fled into the desert with very few provisions.

   1. Often, when we run from what we perceive to be a desperate situation, what we first thought was a good idea turns out to be a terrible idea. This was the case for Hagar.

   2. It is hard to understand how Abraham and Sarah could allow this situation to happen. But people do all kinds of cruel things to each other because we live in a fallen world where the devil roams around seeking to kill and destroy people (see John 10:10).

II. Does God see everybody all at the same time or just civilizations in general?

   A. The Bible indicates that God interacts with people on an absolutely personal basis.

   1. "For God so loved the world that he gave his one and only Son" (John 3:16). God sent his Son into the world so everyone on earth could know him as a father.

   2. A person who believes in Jesus is restored perfectly back to the Father (see John 11:25–26), which indicates that God is quite personal.

3. No matter how hopeless our situation seems, and no matter where we find ourselves, we can trust that God not only sees us but also never leaves us.

B. There is something in this earth called "free will." God gave humans the ability to choose him, which means they have the ability to choose all kinds of things.

1. In a free-will society, people destroy each other, hurt each other, and do terrible things to one another. But this does not mean that God does not care, and it does not mean that he will not intervene. We again see this at work in the story of Hagar.

2. Hagar's life was not considered to be valuable in her society, but her life was absolutely valuable to God. The enemy would love for us all to believe that God has forgotten us, but he is always with us.

C. When God created Adam, he "breathed into his nostrils the breath of life" (Genesis 2:7).

1. This does not mean we are God but rather that God has placed his Spirit within us. When we believe in Jesus, there can be no separation between us and God. We are made in God's image.

2. The Hebrew word *demut* is often translated in English as "likeness." But the image in the Hebrew is of a shadow. So being made in the image of God means that we are a shadow of God. We cannot separate ourselves from our shadow—we just don't see it when we're not standing in the sun.

3. The fact that God sees us as valuable and made in his image also means that he is never too busy for us. He always has time for us. We are always worthy of his attention.

III. What can we draw from Hagar's story and apply to our own lives?

   A. The story of Hagar contains many promises for us today.

   1. Isaiah wrote, "Have you not known? Have you not heard? The LORD is the everlasting God, the Creator of the ends of the earth. He does not faint or grow weary" (Isaiah 40:28 ESV). The Lord did not grow weary in Hagar's day, and he does not grow weary today.

   2. Isaiah continued, "His understanding is unsearchable. He gives power to the faint, and to him who has no might he increases strength" (Isaiah 40:28–29 ESV). The Lord gave power to Hagar and increased her strength in her situation with Abraham and Sarah.

   B. God sent Hagar back to a place of suffering—back to Abraham and Sarah. In our lives, we don't want God to say this to us.

   1. But God took away Hagar's shame—he took away her slavery—and said that he had seen her in her suffering. God also promised Hagar that she would leave a legacy through her descendants.

   2. No matter what our lives look like right now, we all have a legacy to leave behind. God has predestined each of us to be here on this earth at this exact period in time.

Ishmael in Jewish Tradition

In the biblical story, we learn that Ishmael was the son of Abraham and Hagar, born when Abraham was eighty-six years of age. God had promised Abraham that "a son who is your own flesh and blood will be your heir" (Genesis 15:4) and that this child would come through Sarah (see 17:16). Isaac, born of Abraham and Sarah, was the son of God's promise, and the one through whom the Lord would extend his covenant to his people (see 21:12).

But this does not mean that Ishmael was left out of God's plans. The Lord promised that Ishmael would also have descendants "too numerous to count" (16:10) and that he would make Ishmael "into a nation" (21:13) because he was Abraham's offspring. After Ishmael was forced to leave his father's home, he dwelt in the Desert of Paran, became an archer, took an Egyptian wife, and indeed had many sons (see 21:20–21; 25:12–18). He reunited at least once with Isaac when their father died, burying Abraham in a cave alongside Sarah (see 25:9).

Outside of this biblical account, we find stories in Jewish tradition that Abraham tried to raise up Ishmael in righteousness but, true to God's prophecy, the boy remained an idolatrous "wild donkey of a man" (16:12). Rabbi Simeon ben Yohai, writing in the second century AD, stated that the nature of Ishmael's "mocking" of Isaac (21:9) was against those who claimed that Isaac would be Abraham's chief heir. Ishmael instead asserted that he, as the firstborn son, would receive two-thirds of his father's inheritance according to the customs of the day.[12]

The Roman historian Josephus, writing in the first century AD, stated that Sarah "at first loved Ishmael . . . with an affection not inferior to that to a son of her own." However, after the birth of Isaac, she worried the older body would "do him injuries when their father should be dead," and so persuaded Abraham to send Hagar and Ishmael away. After God revealed the well to Hagar, the mother and son met with some shepherds, who cared for them. Josephus concludes his account by stating that Ishmael's descendants "inhabited all the country from Euphrates, to the Red Sea: and called it Nabatene. They are an Arabian nation."[13]

3. It was Mordecai who said to Esther, "And who knows but that you have come to your royal position for such a time as this?" (Esther 4:14). Our destiny is great in God.

IV. What can we surmise happened to Hagar when she went back?

A. The stories in the Bible can frustrate us because they leave many questions unanswered. We simply don't know what happened to Hagar and Ishmael when they went back.

1. We don't know if Hagar reconciled with Abraham and Sarah. We know that years later when Isaac was born, she and Ishmael were sent away (see Genesis 21:8–21).

2. But we can surmise that after Hagar encountered the living God, her life was never the same. From that time on, she knew that she could go to God, because he had seen her, and that he would meet her in her need. They had a *relationship*—not religion.

B. When we have an encounter with God, it transforms everything about the way we think.

1. The Greek word *metanoia* means "to repent." Many people think *repent* means to have guilt. But it actually means "to turn around" and go back to what is right.

2. Jesus taught us to repent and come back to God. When we do, we are welcomed back just as the prodigal son was welcomed back by his father (see Luke 15:22–24).

C. Hagar likely had a difficult time when she returned to Abraham and Sarah. We can't imagine all the ups and downs that she would have endured. But we do know that God would have given her strength.

1. Paul wrote that God said to him, "My grace is sufficient for you, for my power is made perfect in weakness" (2 Corinthians 12:9). When Hagar was in her weakest moments—which must have happened again and again—she could rely on God's strength.

2. The prophet Isaiah wrote, "Do not fear, for I [God] am with you; do not be dismayed, for I am your God" (Isaiah 41:10). Hagar said, "God, you saw me . . . you are my God."

3. Isaiah continued, "I [God] will strengthen you and help you; I will uphold you with my righteous right hand" (Isaiah 41:10). The right arm of God, when it is bare, represents God as the warrior—the God who fights on behalf of his people.

4. Isaiah concluded, "For I am the LORD your God who takes hold of your right hand" (Isaiah 41:13). Jesus sits at the right hand of the Father, the "warrior arm" of God, because he is the one who finished the war. We do not fight *for* victory but *from* victory.

Discuss | 35 minutes

Take some time to discuss what you just watched by answering the following questions. There are some suggested questions below to help you begin your discussion, but feel free to pick any of the additional questions as time allows.

Suggested Questions

1. Hagar was Egyptian, which meant she was an outsider. She was a woman, which meant she didn't have rights. She was also a slave, which meant she could not improve her situation. What do you think life was like for her in Abraham's family? What does it say about God that he spoke to her in spite of these "strikes" against her?

2. Read Psalm 33:13–15. God in Scripture is portrayed as *omnipresent*, which means that he has the ability to be present with everyone at all times. What does this psalm say that God does concerning humankind? Why is it important for us followers of Christ—as God's children—to know we have a heavenly Father who sees and hears us?

3. When we look at the story of Hagar, we see that God "gives strength to the weary and increases the power of the weak" (Isaiah 40:29). How did God give his strength to Hagar? What are some of God's promises to you that you can take from her story?

4. In Acts 3:19, Peter said to a crowd in Jerusalem, "Repent, then, and turn to God, so that your sins may be wiped out." In the Bible, to *repent* means "to turn from" or "to

change one's mind." How does this differ from just having guilt for your sin? What does God promise to do when people change their mind about sin and return to him?

Additional Questions

5. Read aloud Ephesians 2:1–2. In this passage, the apostle Paul describes the reality of the world in which we live. Satan is the "prince" or "ruler" of this earth, which means he has some power (given to him by God) to influence people for his purposes. How do we see Satan at work in Hagar's story? How do we know, based on her story, that God has greater power?

6. God has given humans *free will*, which means every person has the choice to obey him or disobey him. In Hagar's story, this meant Sarah had the choice to mistreat Hagar, and Abraham had the choice to remove himself from the situation and ignore what was happening. Given this, why do you think God still allows us to have free will?

7. Paul wrote, "Be joyful in hope, patient in affliction, faithful in prayer" (Romans 12:12). In Hagar's story, the Lord asked her to be patient in her affliction and return to the situation that she had just fled. What are some of the ways that you have been "patient in affliction" in your life? How did you encounter God during those times?

8. Read Colossians 2:13–15. How does this passage support the idea that as followers of Jesus, we do not fight *for* victory but *from* a place of victory?

Respond | 10 minutes

Review the outline for the video teaching and any notes you took. In the space below, write down your most significant takeaway from this session.

Pray | 10 minutes

End your time by praying together, asking God to provide his strength whenever you are feeling weak. Ask if anyone has any prayer requests to share. Write those requests down in the space below so you and your group members can pray about them in the week ahead.

Name   Request

Personal Study

As you discussed this week, God makes no distinctions between people when it comes to those he uses in his plans. As the apostle Paul wrote, "God does not show favoritism" (Romans 2:11). Hagar was a foreigner (an Egyptian) and had a lowly position (a slave), yet God chose to reveal himself to her. She was even the first person in Scripture to give him a name! Hagar's story reveals that regardless of our position in life, we can be assured that God always sees us. As you explore these themes in the story of Hagar this week, be sure to write down your responses to the questions in the spaces provided, as you will be given a few minutes to share your insights at the start of the next session if you are doing this study with others. If you are reading *The God of the Way* alongside this study, first review pages 126–134 in chapter 9 of the book.

— Day 1 —

Never Abandoned

Hagar is introduced in the Bible as an Egyptian slave (Genesis 16:1). As such, she was in the lowest social class and had no rights. Even the child she had with Abraham could be considered Sarah's and not Hagar's. This is likely why Sarah arranged for Hagar to be her surrogate.[14]

Our world has a long and painful history with slavery—and one that continues to this day. Enslaved people back in Hagar's day, just as now, were not treated as fully human. They were not considered a part of society but merely served it. Hagar entered Sarah's household with this status—bought and sold. She was likely not given a choice to be Sarah's surrogate but simply had to do what her mistress told her. When she did fulfill her duty, Sarah treated her so badly that she ran away.

Hagar was abandoned by the world and everyone in it. This is why her story is so miraculous when we read about it in the Bible. Even though she had been abandoned by *everyone* she had ever known, she was not abandoned by God. Instead, her story—an enslaved person's story—is elevated in the pages of Scripture. We know her name. We know her son's name. And we find solace in her tale. We can see ourselves in her desperate cries in the wilderness.

We have all felt abandoned, whether that was by a parent, a spouse, a best friend, or someone else who was close to us. Maybe you have even felt abandoned by God. We all know the sting of rejection, of being left alone, of not being cared for in the way we need. The world can feel like a lonely place. But this is when we need to remember God's character as displayed in Hagar's story. He did not abandon Hagar, and he will not abandon us. He revealed this to us when he sent his Son, Jesus, to take on human flesh and make his dwelling among us in this world (see John 1:14).

This ultimate display of devotion proves that no matter who you are, no matter your social status or class, you are never abandoned. God is always with you.

Read | Deuteronomy 31:7–8 and Matthew 28:18–20

Reflect

1. Moses encouraged Joshua to be strong and courageous in the passage from Deuteronomy shortly after naming the younger man as his successor. Clearly, Joshua had big shoes to fill, and he probably needed the encouragement. Moses would not be with him much longer, but God would. How does Moses describe God in verse 8? From what you know about Moses, why do you think he was able to speak of God in this way?

2. Jesus gave his disciples the parting words recorded in the passage in the Gospel of Matthew after his resurrection and before he ascended back into heaven. What promise did Jesus give to them at this time? How do you think this promise made the disciples feel—especially as Jesus was about to leave them?

3. When have you felt abandoned? How did this abandonment affect the way you viewed yourself, your relationships with others, and God? Why is abandonment so painful?

4. Even though Hagar was a foreigner and an enslaved person, the Bible records her name, her son's name, and even provides a list of her descendants (see Genesis 25:12–18). What does this say about how God saw her worth and value?

Pray | Be honest with God in your prayer time. Tell him how and when you have felt abandoned, whether that experience was years ago or yesterday. Thank him for being a God who does not abandon his people. Ask him for a reminder of his presence today.

Day 2

Surrender to God

Surrender. What comes to mind when you hear that word? We all have different relationships with the idea of surrender. Maybe we were forced to surrender something we loved due to life's circumstances—a dream, money, or a job. Or maybe we chose to surrender for the sake of a loved one—a child, a spouse, or a parent. In such cases, the surrender was hard but worth it.

The Christian life requires us to daily surrender our will to God. This is not always easy to do, especially when the path before us is unclear. Surrendering to God can feel like a risk. Hagar must have felt this way during her first experience in the wilderness when the Lord asked her to go back to her mistress "and submit to her" (Genesis 16:9). *Really?* she must have thought. *Submit to Sarah? The one who forced me to be her surrogate and then mistreated me to the point that I had to flee to the wilderness, pregnant and alone? Why should I have to submit to someone like her?*

In order for Hagar to do what God was instructing her to do, she first had to submit her will to the Lord. She had to trust that God knew what he was doing by sending her back to Abraham and Sarah and that he had good plans for her life. She had trust in what he promised next: "You will give birth to a son. You shall name him Ishmael, for the LORD has heard of your misery" (verse 11).

Hagar's story is a complicated one and can easily be equated to God instructing a person to return to an abuser or an abusive situation.[15] But the Bible is clear that God does not condone the abuse of women or of slaves. God was not calling Hagar to submit to *Sarah* but to *him*, because he had a plan for her life that was better than anything she could have imagined. He assured her of this plan. He called her by name. He told her that he had seen her misery.

Because of this, even if Hagar knew that she could not trust her mistress, Sarah, she knew that she could trust the Lord God.

Read | Psalm 37:1–6

Reflect

1. David, the author of this psalm, was a man who had many enemies and a man who was called to surrender to God's call as the leader of Israel. According to verses 1–2, why didn't David need to "fret" or worry about his enemies? What comes to mind when you think about the "safe pasture" that David describes in verse 3?

2. According to verses 5–6, what will happen if we commit our way to God and trust him? What does it mean for you to "commit your way to the LORD"?

3. When is a time in your life that God has called you to surrender your will to his and follow his plans? Did you trust God in making this surrender? Why or why not?

4. What might God be calling you to surrender in your life today? Are you resistant to this surrender or open and willing to do as God asks? Explain your answer.

Pray | What is God telling you today? What is he asking you to surrender? Why can you trust him in this matter? Express any tension you feel with surrendering to God. Ask him to help you trust him in every area of life, knowing that what he has for you on the other side is better.

-Day 3-

From Despair to Joy

Hagar's second trip into the desert was initially as disheartening as her first. After the birth of Isaac, Sarah told Abraham, "Get rid of that slave woman and her son, for that woman's son will never share in the inheritance with my son Isaac" (Genesis 21:10). Even though God had promised Hagar some years before that he would increase her descendants "so much that they will be too numerous to count" (16:10), she must have entered into the desert of Beersheba wondering what had happened to that promise.

When Hagar then ran out of water, the promise from God must have seemed to her to completely disappear. After all, how could her son's lineage become a great nation if he died of thirst in the wilderness?

The Bible says that Hagar was so filled with despair at these events that "she began to sob" (21:16). Her joy had turned into despair in a moment. The same can happen in our lives. One minute everything seems so full of promise—a happy family, a good job, stable relationships—and the next minute everything seems to have turned upside down. When we have experienced this enough times in life, it can be hard to feel joy even in the happy times. Who knows when the other shoe will drop?

But when we journey with God, just as joy can turn to despair on a dime, so can despair turn to joy in an instant. Even in a place like the desert. *El Roi* saw Ishmael and Hagar yet again. He reiterated his promise of inheritance to Ishmael. He offered water to the thirsty duo. In a moment, Hagar's life went from one filled with despair to one filled with promise. Her son would not die. He had a future, the one that was promised to him years before. Despite the threat of Ishmael's inheritance being taken, God was saying that all was not lost. The best was yet to come.

Bad things can—and do—happen to us at any time. But good, unexpected gifts from God can also be given at any time. The despair we feel today will not last forever. When we serve the God Who Sees, our despair will always turn to joy.

Read | Genesis 21:15–21 and Psalm 30:11–12

Reflect

1. God told Hagar not to be afraid, for he heard her son's cries and would "make him into a great nation" (verse 18). According to verses 20–21, where did Ishmael grow up, and what became of him? How did God provide for him and watch over him?

2. In the passage from Psalm 30, the author refers to *sackcloth*, which in those days was a rough fabric worn during times of mourning and distress or to show repentance and humility.[16] How did the Lord dramatically change the psalmist's circumstances in this passage? How did the author of this psalm say that he responded?

3. When is a time in your life that your circumstances changed suddenly for the better? How did you respond to God in that moment?

4. What situation in your life (or in the world) causes you to feel despair? What hope do you have, if any, that God can turn your "wailing into dancing"?

Pray | Read through Psalm 30:11–12 again as your prayer today. Ask God to turn your mourning into dancing and replace your sackcloth with gladness. Praise him for all the times that he has revealed himself in the past and come through for you. Expect him to do it again.

-Day 4-

God Fights for Us

We are taught in this world to be fighters. We fight for our freedom. We fight for our rights. We fight to be heard and seen. Grit and stamina are useful traits to possess. Yet life with God promotes a different posture. With God, we can put down our fists. We can release the need, the desire, to fight. Why? Because God fights *for* us.

We see this in the story of Hagar. When she was dismissed by Abraham and Sarah and suddenly cast out of the family, she did not fight her way back. She probably had no fight left in her! Instead, it was *God* who fought on her behalf. He said to her, "I will increase your descendants so much that they will be too numerous to count" (Genesis 16:10). *Who* would increase her descendants? *God* would. Hagar did not have to do anything.

Throughout the Bible, we see God taking up his people's cause and fighting for them. He fought for the Israelites as they fled from Egypt (see Exodus 14). He fought for his people when they entered into the promised land (see Joshua 6). He fought for his people on King Jehoshaphat's behalf, defeating the Ammonites and Moabites (see 2 Chronicles 20).

Of course, God fought the ultimate battle on behalf of his people when he sent his only Son into the world to pay the price of our sin. Jesus died on a cross, defeated death, and was raised to life so that we might live—a battle we could not have possibly fought on our own. So whatever battle you are facing today, know this: *you don't have to fight it on your own.* You don't have to white-knuckle it. You don't have to work your way to the top. You don't have to prove yourself. Your battle belongs to the Lord, and he will fight for you.

Read | Exodus 14:1–22 and 1 Corinthians 15:54–58

Reflect

1. God had miraculously delivered the Israelites from 400 years of slavery in Egypt. He had called up Moses to serve as their leader and spokesperson and sent a series of

plagues against the Egyptians to force Pharaoh to allow them to leave. The people must have assumed they were safe as they marched away from Egypt, but Pharaoh came after them with his chariots. How did the Israelites respond when they saw Pharaoh's army? What accusations did they level at Moses for leading them to that place?

2. Moses assured the people, "You will see the deliverance the LORD will bring you today. . . . The LORD will fight for you" (Exodus 14:13–14). How did God bring about the Israelites' deliverance? What did God say the Egyptians would realize about him?

3. Paul writes in 1 Corinthians 15:54 that "death has been swallowed up in victory." What does *death* represent in this passage? How did Jesus give us victory over death?

4. What are some of the battles that you have been fighting in your own strength? How do these passages reassure you that you can surrender these battles to the Lord?

Pray | During your prayer time, meditate on these words from Moses: "The LORD will fight for you; you need only be still" (Exodus 14:14). Be still and let this truth sink in. The Lord will fight for you! Choose to surrender your battles to him and trust that he will work on your behalf.

– Day 5 –

The Right Hand of God

Have you ever watched a football game in which you already knew the outcome? Maybe you recorded the event and then someone spoiled the surprise by telling you that your team had won. As you watched the game, you were not worried when your quarterback threw an interception, or your team fumbled, or the opposing team scored. No, you knew that whatever happened, your team would ultimately pull out the victory.

In a similar way, those who have put their faith in Yeshua are watching a "game" that has already been decided. When Jesus died on the cross for our sins, he defeated the enemy once and for all. He completely (and eternally) secured the victory over Satan. This means that we, as his faithful followers, are not fighting *for* victory but *from* a place of victory.

As you learned this week, whenever God mentions his "right hand" in Scripture, he is referring to himself as a warrior—a warrior who fights on our behalf (see Isaiah 41:10, 13). When the New Testament writers refer to Jesus' place in heaven, they likewise say that he is seated at the right hand of the Father (see Acts 2:33; Hebrews 8:1; 1 Peter 3:22). He is seated at God's right hand, symbolizing that the battle has already been won.

What a difference it would make if we lived from a place of believing the battle has been won rather than fighting for the victory on our own! It would be like watching the replay of that football game. We would understand that regardless of the twists and turns, our team will prevail. If we approached life in this manner, we wouldn't worry when things took a turn. We would trust in Jesus' victory and know the outcome has been decided.

Read | 2 Corinthians 12:6–10

Reflect

1. There has been much debate about what the "thorn" that Paul refers to in this passage represents. Some have speculated it is a sin pattern, a difficult relationship, or

the persecution he endured as a Jewish Christ-follower. We don't know for sure, but what we do know is how Paul decided to approach that thorn. In what way did the apostle deal with the thorn in his flesh? How did Jesus respond to Paul's plea?

2. "But he said to me, 'My grace is sufficient for you, for my power is made perfect in weakness'" (verse 9). What does it mean that Jesus' grace is sufficient for us? How is his power made perfect in the midst of our weakness?

3. Paul writes, "When I am weak, then I am strong" (verse 10). In what ways have you seen God use an area of weakness in your life to reveal his supernatural strength?

4. How would your life change if you operated from the mindset that you do not fight *for* victory but *from* a place of victory? What would it take for you to always think that way?

Pray | Pray to Jesus, who is even now seated at the right hand of the Father. Imagine him there in all his victory and glory. Surrender your fight to him. Let yourself be weak. Ask God to help you find rest and grace in that weakness and to help you believe your battle is already won.

For Next Week

Before you meet again with your group, read pages 135–144 in chapter 10 of *The God of the Way*. Also go back and complete any of the study and reflection questions from this personal study that you weren't able to finish.

WEEK 3

BEFORE GROUP MEETING	Read pages 135–144 in chapter 10 of *The God of the Way* Read the Welcome section (page 55)
GROUP MEETING	Discuss the Connect questions Watch the video teaching for session 3 Discuss the questions that follow as a group Do the closing exercise and pray (pages 55–66)
PERSONAL STUDY – DAY 1	Complete the daily study (pages 68–69)
PERSONAL STUDY – DAY 2	Complete the daily study (pages 70–71)
PERSONAL STUDY – DAY 3	Complete the daily study (pages 72–73)
PERSONAL STUDY – DAY 4	Complete the daily study (pages 74–75)
PERSONAL STUDY – DAY 5 (before week 4 group meeting)	Complete the daily study (pages 76–77) Read pages 144–151 in chapter 10 of *The God of the Way* Complete any unfinished personal studies

Ruth

GOD REDIRECTS OUR LIVES

"Look," said Naomi, "your sister-in-law is going back to her people and her gods. Go back with her." But Ruth replied, "Don't urge me to leave you or to turn back from you. Where you go I will go, and where you stay I will stay. Your people will be my people and your God my God. Where you die I will die, and there I will be buried. May the LORD deal with me, be it ever so severely, if even death separates you and me."

RUTH 1:15–17

The Land of Moab

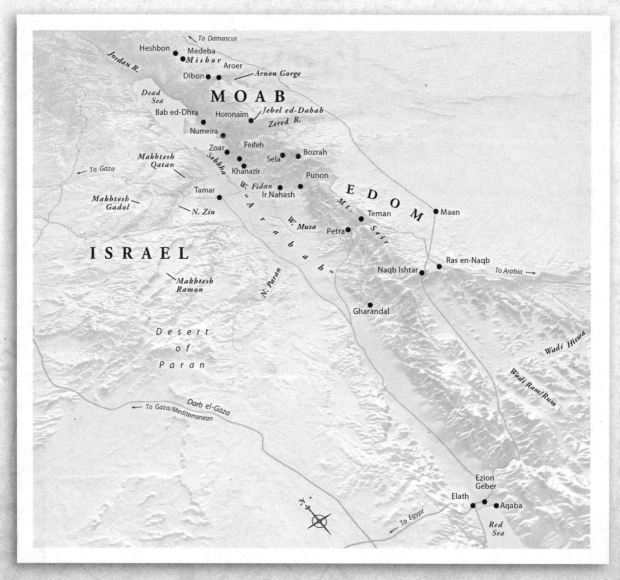

Welcome | Read On Your Own

In the last session, you saw how God revealed himself to Hagar on two occasions when she found herself on an unexpected journey out in the desert. You looked at how God sees *everyone*—regardless of their status or position in life—on a personal and individual basis. You saw that Hagar's story contains many promises for you today, such as the fact that God will be with you in difficult times of suffering and give you strength to persevere.

Another woman in the Bible who found herself on an unexpected journey was an Israelite named Naomi. Her story takes places centuries later "in the days when the judges ruled" over the twelve tribes (Ruth 1:1). Naomi and her husband, Elimelek, were from the town of Bethlehem, but a famine in the land of Judah forced them to travel to the neighboring country of Moab, where there was food. The Israelites and Moabites had a long history of enmity between them, so Naomi was very much living in enemy territory.

Unfortunately, the situation for Naomi only grew worse once she was settled in Moab. Her husband died, followed by the deaths ten years later of her two sons. Suddenly, Naomi was faced with the daunting task of trying to survive in a patriarchal society where women had few rights and fewer ways to support themselves. She deemed that her chances to do this would be better back in her home country and set out for Bethlehem. It was a journey into the unknown . . . but fortunately not a journey she would have to take alone.

In this session, you will take a closer look at Ruth, the daughter-in-law of Naomi who doggedly refused to abandon her on the road to Bethlehem. She and Naomi were not a likely pair. But their unusual partnership would prove to be their saving grace.

Connect | 15 minutes

Welcome to session 3 of *The God Who Sees*. To get things started for this week's group time, discuss one of the following questions:

- What is a key insight or takeaway from last week's personal study that you would like to share with the group?

— *or* —

- Think of someone in your life who demonstrates character, integrity, and faithfulness. What does that person do that you especially admire?

Watch | 20 minutes

Now watch the video for this session. As you watch, use the following outline to record any thoughts or concepts that stand out to you.

I. What is the setting of the story of Ruth in the Bible—and why is her story important?

    A. Ruth's story is an intimate human story with global repercussions. It reveals that we never know who God will use or what he will do when we are open to his plans.

        1. Ruth is a small book in the Bible, appearing immediately after the book of Judges. So we might be tempted to think of the book of Ruth as insignificant and just "move on."

        2. But Ruth's story is a powerful testimony of what can happen—and what God will do—when one person chooses to be faithful to another person.

        3. The story is even more remarkable when we consider that Ruth was an outsider. She was from Moab, modern-day Jordan, which in that day was worlds away from Israel.

    B. As the story opens, we learn that Naomi and her husband, Elimelek, were from Bethlehem, and yet they ended up in the land of Moab.

        1. There is a famine in Israel, so Naomi and Elimelech move their family to Moab so they will not starve to death. Their sons, Mahlon and Kilion, go with them. They settle there, and the sons marry women from Moab: Orpah and Ruth (see Ruth 1:1–4).

        2. The Israelites and Moabites were ancient enemies. The animosity traced back to when Moses was leading the Israelites through the wilderness and a Moabite king named Balak summoned a prophet-for-hire named Balaam to put a curse on God's people (see Numbers 22:4–7).

The Land of Moab

"In the days when the judges ruled, there was a famine in the land. So a man from Bethlehem in Judah, together with his wife and two sons, went to live for a while in the country of Moab" (Ruth 1:1). This opening to the book of Ruth establishes the date in which the events took place (c. 1100 BC) and the setting for the story (Moab). But what do we know about that nation?

Location. Moab was located along the eastern shore of the Dead Sea on a plateau between the Arnon and Zered rivers in what today is the country of Jordan. The people of Moab primarily grew wheat and barley and used the soil for pasture-land (according to 2 Kings 3:4–5, one king of Moab named Mesha raised sheep). There were deep ravines to the north of the country as well as Mount Nebo, where Moses died (see Deuteronomy 34:1–8).[17]

History. According to Genesis 19:37–38, the Moabites descended from an incestuous relationship between Lot and his oldest daughter. When the Israelites under Moses defeated the Amorites, a panicked King Balak of Moab summoned a prophet-for-hire named Balaam to put a curse on them (see Numbers 22:6). Balaam was unable to do so, but the invasion King Balak feared did not come. Instead, the Israelites settled near Shittim and sinned against God by intermingling with the Moabites (see Numbers 25:1–2). In the time of the judges, King Eglon of Moab invaded Israel and conquered as far as Jericho (see Judges 3:12–14).[18]

Language. The Moabite language was related to Hebrew, Ammonite, and Edomite. Most of what is known about it comes from the discovery of the Mesha Stele, a stone slab dated to 840 BC that contains Moabite text in the name of King Mesha.[19]

Religion. The Moabites worshiped many gods, but the chief deity was Chemosh (see Numbers 21:29). The Moabites would engage in human sacrifices, especially in battle to secure a favorable outcome (see 2 Kings 3:27). The Mesha Stele also mentions a female deity named Ashtar-Chemosh and a male god named Nebo (possibly the Babylonian god Nabu).[20]

3. The Moabites would not have been welcomed into Israel. They were actually forbidden from entering into the Israelites' worship of God (see Deuteronomy 23:3).

4. Ruth married into Naomi and Elimelek's family, so their God became her God. But this did not mean that she would have been welcomed into Israelite society.

C. Naomi's husband dies in Moab, followed by the deaths of both of her sons.

1. We do not know why Elimelek and the sons die. But their deaths mean that Naomi, Ruth, and Orpah are now left on their own to fend for themselves (see Ruth 1:5).

2. Naomi learns the famine in Israel has ended and decides to go back to Bethlehem. She tells Orpah and Ruth to stay with their people (see Ruth 1:6–13).

3. Orpah goes back to Moab, and not one mention is made of her again in Scripture. But Ruth refuses to leave and accompanies Naomi to Bethlehem (see Ruth 1:14–18).

II. What was unique about Naomi and Ruth's relationship, and what challenges did they face?

A. Moab was a polytheistic world, but Ruth had married into a family that believed in just the one true God. She knew God—Jehovah God—when she came with Naomi to Bethlehem.

1. What is fascinating is that the text reveals these two women forged an alliance—to the point where Ruth would look to Naomi when she made her decisions.

2. The terrain the women crossed would have been rough. It is beautiful there, but not a route that anyone would have wanted to traverse—especially in the heat.

3. In addition, they were two women traveling alone. There were marauders in that region. Naomi and Ruth had only each other as they trudged along on the journey.

B. The relationship between Ruth and Naomi is like the relationship that God has with us.

1. Of course, we know that Ruth and Naomi's relationship was *not* perfect. Whenever women who are related hang out together for a long time . . . it can't be perfect!

2. But the women had incredible love for each other. The picture of the two of them is representative of the word *hesed* in Hebrew, meaning "loyal" or "faithful loving-kindness."

3. *Hesed* repents God's love toward us. But it goes deeper, because God sent his only Son to lay down his life for us so that we could have abundant life and be set free (see John 8:36; 10:10).

C. When Ruth told Naomi, "Your people will be my people and your God my God" (Ruth 1:16), she meant that she was never turning back. She displayed tremendous integrity.

1. If Naomi did not have Ruth—coming into a land where she was too old to have value and not being able to own property—she would likely have starved.

2. If Ruth did not have Naomi—coming into Israel as a despised Moabitess—she would not have survived. She needed to be with someone who was originally from that land.

3. Both women were also going into the unknown. Naomi didn't know if the famine had killed everyone who was once in her family. Both were entering into uncharted territory.

III. What is a *kinsman-redeemer* and what impact does it have on Ruth and Naomi's story?

A. In the culture of the day, the man was the rescuer. So the law of Moses stipulated a male "kinsman-redeemer" could redeem the life of a female relative (see Leviticus 25:25).

1. Ruth would not have been eligible to have a kinsman-redeemer because she was not from Israel. This would not have been an option had she not been in Naomi's family.

2. Naomi also could not have a kinsman-redeemer because she was too old and had no property for a relative to inherit. The kinsman-redeemer would either have heirs with the woman he was rescuing or inherit property from the woman's deceased husband.

3. In that time, women could not own property. So if a woman inherited land from her husband and that husband died, the male kinsman-redeemer would come in and manage all her affairs. The woman was stuck with nothing, while the male got everything.

B. Naomi had nothing and could not bear children, so she couldn't have a kinsman-redeemer. But Ruth, since she was in her family, *was* eligible for a kinsman-redeemer.

1. The narrative of Ruth is powerful because it reveals that God undermines everything the enemy wants to do. The *hesed* of God saved Ruth and Naomi.

2. The story also reveals the power of steadfastness, loyalty, faithfulness, determination, tenacity, and boldness. Ruth and Naomi gained courage from each other.

Gleaning in Biblical Times

"Ruth the Moabite said to Naomi, 'Let me go to the fields and pick up the leftover grain behind anyone in whose eyes I find favor'" (Ruth 2:2). When Ruth accompanied Naomi back to the land of Israel, she knew that she would have to do something to support the two of them if they were to survive. The strategy that she proposed to do this was known as *gleaning*.

Gleaning was the means by which God ensured the poor among his people—like Ruth and Naomi—could secure enough food in order to live. Under the law of Moses, the landowners were to leave a portion of their fields unharvested and also not have their workers pick up whatever fell to the ground. The rules applied to vineyards as well: "When you reap the harvest of your land, do not reap to the very edges of your field or gather the gleanings of your harvest. Do not go over your vineyard a second time or pick up the grapes that have fallen. Leave them for the poor and the foreigner. I am the LORD your God" (Leviticus 19:9–10).[21]

The amount of grain (or grapes) the workers were to leave behind seems to have been up to the landowner to decide. So it was that in Ruth's case, Boaz instructed his workers to pull extra "stalks for her from the bundles and leave them for her to pick up" (Ruth 2:16). They were also not to rebuke her, which indicates that those who had to resort to these extreme measures to survive were often looked on with scorn. Boaz made it clear to his workers that they were not to scorn Ruth but do everything possible to lighten her task.[22]

These laws concerning gleaning were necessary because every family in Israel (with the exception of the priests) was to have an allotment of land that remained in the family. "No inheritance in Israel is to pass from one tribe to another, for every Israelite shall keep the tribal inheritance of their ancestors" (Numbers 36:7). In this way, everyone in Israel had the means to grow food. But foreigners (like Ruth), widows (like Naomi), and orphans did not receive an inheritance of land, and thus they were the most susceptible to poverty in Israelite society. Gleaning gave those who found themselves in this situation at least a chance to secure food.[23]

IV. What was the plan that Naomi put together to secure a kinsman-redeemer?

    A. When the women arrived in Bethlehem, they knew they needed a plan. So Ruth ended up going out into a field of one of Naomi's relatives and gleaning (see Ruth 2:1–2).

        1. Gleaning was a practice that allowed a person to go into a recently harvested field and pick up whatever grain remained (see Leviticus 19:9–10). Ruth became one of the needy going around and collecting enough food so her family would not starve to death.

        2. Naomi's relative who owned the field was Boaz. When he saw Ruth, he realized she was a good woman and wanted to help her. He also invited her to share a meal (see Ruth 2:3–16).

        3. This is symbolic of how Jesus said, "Come to the banqueting table and dine" (see Luke 14:15–24). Boaz invites Ruth to be part of his culture. This is what Jesus says—"Come be part of the kingdom." It is such a beautiful representation of acceptance.

    B. Naomi hears about the favor that Boaz has shown to Ruth and soon forms a plan (see Ruth 2:19–23).

        1. Naomi teaches Ruth how to present herself in the culture of the day—symbolically, how she can present herself as one who is available to be redeemed by a kinsman-redeemer. She then instructs Ruth to go to Boaz's threshing floor during harvest time to enact the plan (see Ruth 3:1–4).

2. Naomi's instructions have to do with Ruth presenting herself as one who is in need and one who wants to be assimilated into the culture.

3. Naomi knows that Boaz has already accepted Ruth at his table. He has given her more grain in the fields to take home. His favor is already on her.

C. Ruth goes to the threshing floor, lies at Boaz's feet, and uncovers them. The Bible tells us that in the middle of the night, Boaz wakes and finds her there (see Ruth 3:7–8).

1. Ruth's act of uncovering Boaz's feet is symbolic of her asking him to "cover" her—to cover her with his life, protect her, marry her.

2. This is the way marriage proposals were done . . . but probably not ever before in this manner. Ruth pretty much established this way of doing it.

3. No one would have dreamed at the time that Ruth would play such a pivotal role in the history of the church—and the history of the world. Jesus, the Messiah, never would have come to earth the way he did if it had not been for Ruth and Boaz.

D. Perhaps the greatest lesson we can learn from Ruth and Naomi's lives is that no matter how bleak it looks, when we stick together and include God, we become undefeatable.

Discuss | 35 minutes

Take some time to discuss what you just watched by answering the following questions. There are some suggested questions below to help you begin your discussion, but feel free to pick any of the additional questions as time allows.

Suggested Questions

1. Naomi's story is filled with tragedy. A famine forces her to flee to an enemy nation to survive. Her husband dies there, followed by the death of her two sons. When she returns to Bethlehem, she tells the women, "Call me Mara, because the Almighty has made my life very bitter" (Ruth 1:20). What does this say about how Naomi viewed her future? When have you responded to the misfortunes in your life in this way?

2. The Hebrew word *hesed* not only describes qualities such as love, mercy, compassion, loyalty, and faithfulness but also implies an action taken on behalf of another person in need.[24] How does this understanding of *hesed* describe the relationship Ruth and Naomi had? How does *hesed* describe God's relationship with us (see Romans 5:8)?

3. When you look at the story of Ruth and Naomi, what stands out is that both women needed each other to survive. Why would Naomi have struggled when she returned to Israel if she did not have Ruth? Why would Ruth have struggled without Naomi?

4. Read aloud Psalm 91:1–4. When Ruth uncovered Boaz's feet, she was symbolically indicating that she desired him to cover her and protect her. How is this representative of the way that God covers us? What promise is contained for us in this psalm?

Additional Questions

5. It is easy to fault Naomi's daughter-in-laaw Orpah for returning to her home country of Moab, but the reality is that she was only following Naomi's instructions. What stands out is Ruth's refusal to leave *in spite* of her mother-in-law's instructions. What does this reveal about Ruth's character? What lifelong commitment was she making when she refused to turn back to her homeland?

6. Read aloud Ecclesiastes 4:9–12. Ruth and Naomi's relationship illustrates the truth of this passage. What strength did they gain from each other? In what ways were the two stronger together than either of them could have been if they were on their own?

7. The apostle Paul writes, "We know that in all things God works for the good of those who love him, who have been called according to his purpose" (Romans 8:28). How did the Lord ultimately reward Ruth and Naomi's faithfulness to each other? How did God turn a situation that the enemy meant for evil into something very good?

8. When Boaz saw Ruth gleaning in his fields, he invited her to share a meal with him (see Ruth 2:14). In the culture of the day, the act of sharing a meal represented inclusion within the community. How is this a picture of what God does for each of us?

Respond | 10 minutes

Review the outline for the video teaching and any notes you took. In the space below, write down your most significant takeaway from this session.

Pray | 10 minutes

End your time by praying together, thanking God for the faithful people that he has placed in your life. Ask if anyone has any prayer requests to share. Write those requests down in the space below so you and your group members can pray about them in the week ahead.

Name   Request

_____   _____
_____   _____
_____   _____
_____   _____
_____   _____
_____   _____
_____   _____
_____   _____
_____   _____
_____   _____
_____   _____
_____   _____
_____   _____

Personal Study

As you discussed this week, God rewards those who are faithful to him and follow his command to love others (see Matthew 22:37–40). Ruth demonstrated her love for Naomi by refusing to leave her side. Naomi demonstrated her love for Ruth by training her in the customs of Israel. Both women benefited from the relationship, and the God who sees all acts of kindness—no matter how small—blessed their lives. As you explore these themes this week, be sure to write down your responses to the questions in the spaces provided, as you will be given a few minutes to share your insights at the start of the next session. If you are reading *The God of the Way* alongside this study, first review pages 135–144 in chapter 10 of the book.

-Day 1-

Choosing the Future

Maybe you've had this experience. You decided to move to a new city across the country. You said your goodbyes to family and friends, packed your car, and are now driving down the highway. But now, a few hours in, you are beginning to wonder if you're making a mistake. You're not familiar with this new city. You don't know anyone there. Your anxiety increases. Why would you leave the familiar for the unknown? What felt like a good idea a few months ago no longer seems so great. You look in your rearview mirror and consider turning back.

Ruth and Orpah faced this critical decision on the road from Moab to Bethlehem. At one point in the journey, Naomi stopped, turned to them, and said, "Return home, my daughters. Why would you come with me? Am I going to have any more sons, who could become your husbands?" (Ruth 1:11). As we know from the story, Orpah chose to go back to the familiar. But Ruth chose to move into an unknown future and an unfamiliar land.

You don't have to literally move to a new physical place to run into this type of decision. Throughout life, you are given the choice to move forward into the unknown or move backward to the comforts of this past. That past could be a place, an addiction, a toxic relationship. It could be a community you know isn't good for you, a belief system that has hurt you, or a family member who continues to let you down. But even when that past is painful, when that past is what is familiar to you, you will be tempted at times to go back.

Ruth set a courageous example of moving forward in life. Rather than returning to the comfort of her home, her people, and her gods in Moab, she chose to take her chances with Naomi and worship the one true God in the town of Bethlehem. She chose to move forward. She could not have known how greatly God would provide for her there! She could not have known that her decision would put her smack-dab in the middle of Jesus' lineage. She made the decision in faith, trusting that the unknown of her future was better than the comfort of her past.

Read | Proverbs 3:3–6 and Psalm 119:105

Reflect

1. The book of Proverbs, as well as the books Job and Ecclesiastes, falls under a category in the Bible known as "wisdom literature." The author, possibly Solomon, fills his book with bits of knowledge that he wanted to pass on to other people of faith. What does he say will happen when we trust the Lord? How are we supposed to trust the Lord?

2. What does it mean to "bind" love and faithfulness to us and never let them leave us? How did Ruth demonstrate this kind of love and faithfulness?

3. The author of Psalm 119 did not have the Gospels or the New Testament letters. When he refers to "God's word," he means the law or Torah—the books of the Hebrew Bible he would have learned as part of his faith. Considering this, what do you think he means when he says God's word is a lamp for his feet? Notice that the psalmist does not compare God's word to the sun or to a thousand torches—he compares it to a single *lamp*. What does this tell you about the way in which God guides us on our path?

4. When is a time you chose to return to the comforts of the past rather than move forward on the path God provided? What happened as a result?

5. Where do you feel God calling you to move forward today? How do you feel about this— hesitant, unsure, anxious, or perhaps courageous and bold? Explain your answer.

Pray | Turn to God's Word as your guide today, whether it's the passages from today's study or other verses that comfort you in times of the unknown. Choose one passage. What is this scripture saying to you? How has God promised to be with you as you move forward?

– Day 2 –

The Power of *Hesed*

There is a difference between being *nice* and being *kind*. Being nice is saying the right thing, giving a compliment, hosting in the correct manner. Kindness is deeper. To be kind is to be empathetic, genuine, and nonjudgmental. While the words have similar meanings in the dictionary, you can always tell when someone is being nice to you versus kind.

The Hebrew word *hesed* takes this idea of kindness to an even deeper level. As one commentator notes, "A stranger may show kindness, a stranger does not show *hesed*. That is because *hesed* is a covenantal concept, and covenants are not made between strangers. *Hesed* is enduring covenant loyalty and love. It refers to an unwavering commitment and often is used of God's permanent, unchanging love ('steadfast love')."[25] This is the type of kindness displayed between Ruth and Naomi, between Boaz and Ruth, and between God and his people. The word is even used twice by Naomi (see Ruth 1:8) and once by Boaz (see 3:10).

What examples of *hesed* do you have in your life? What type of faithfulness, kindness, and loyalty have you been shown or given to others? Maybe you have this type of relationship with your spouse, your children, or a dear friend. If you do, you recognize that you can't show this type of kindness to everyone! Your energy and love have limits. But fortunately, God's energy and love are limitless. He shows *hesed* to all of his people—a *hesed* embodied through his Son, Jesus, the ultimate display of covenantal love and kindness.[26]

On our worst days, when we've run from God, or we've chosen comfort over God's calling, or we've ignored his Word and gone our own way, God's offer of *hesed* holds true. Jesus' merciful arms remain open. Because a covenant made with God is one made forever.

Read | Ruth 1:16–17 and Psalm 23:1–6

Reflect

1. When Naomi told Ruth that she should return to Moab to be with her people and her gods, Ruth responded with the beautiful promise that we find in verses 16–17.

What do you think inspired Ruth to show this type of covenantal kindness to Naomi? How does this promise that Ruth made show *hesed* to the Lord God?

2. *Hesed* is used 127 times in the Psalms. In Psalm 23, the word *hesed* is translated as *mercy*. According to this psalm, how does God show *hesed* toward us?

3. What relationships in your life display *hesed*, if any? How have you felt *hesed* from this person? How have you displayed *hesed* to him or her? (If you don't have a relationship that models this in your life, where have you seen this in others' relationships?)

4. How have you experienced *hesed* from God? Is it difficult or easy for you to experience God in this way? Explain your answer.

Pray | Thank God for his loving-kindness toward you. Even if you don't feel it from him today, have confidence that it is there, and ask him to help you show this type of kindness to those close to you. Thank him for sending his Son as an embodied example of *hesed*.

-Day 3-

The Servant-Heart of Ruth

We all know *those* type of people . . . the truly servant-hearted types. The ones who from a distance seem too good to be true.

Is she *really* that kind?

Is he *really* that giving?

Some people just seem to possess the gift of service without expecting anything in return. This was certainly true of Ruth. From the first chapter in her story, she models the servant's heart. She serves her mother-in-law, Naomi, and loyally stays by her side. She works in the fields to provide food for them. She does exactly what her mother-in-law tells her to do in regard to Boaz.

Ruth then approaches Boaz with a servant heart. She lies at his feet, according to the custom of the day, and asks for her covering and protection. (She does not demand it.) Ruth's brand of service isn't simply doing what others tell her to do. From her story, we get the sense that she served others out of faithfulness. She trusted Naomi. She trusted Boaz. And she came to trust in the God whom they served.

While we've all come across the rare, truly servant-hearted types, they are just that—*rare*. Most of us struggle with serving others. Our human tendency is to serve ourselves first and others second. We look out for number one: *us*. We've been burned in the past. We've let others go first only to realize that we will never get our turn. We don't trust others. We don't trust God. Life has taught us that we must look out for ourselves.

Ruth could have internalized this message as well. Look at her life. Her husband died. She was a foreigner in a foreign land. But still, she trusted the God of Naomi and Boaz. She put others first, and her circumstances radically changed. Ruth's servant heart did not leave her in the dust. She was not a doormat. No, instead, her servant heart allowed her to be used by God for his greater purposes. Her servant heart is the reason we are still telling her story today.

Read | Proverbs 31:25–31

Reflect

1. In the Hebrew Bible, the book of Proverbs comes directly before the book of Ruth, so the passage above could be understood to describe Ruth.[27] What is the woman in this passage like? Describe her in modern-day terms. How does Ruth embody this image?

2. Why does the author of this passage in Proverbs praise this woman? How does this tend to differ from the other reasons that we praise women in our culture today?

3. Who do you know who is like Ruth or the Proverbs 31 woman—someone who is servant-hearted? How do you feel about this person?

4. How do you personally feel about serving others? Does it come naturally to you or is it much more difficult? Who (and where) do you feel called to serve today?

Pray | Ask God where he could use you in his service today. Ask him to give you the courage, energy, strength, or whatever it is you need to minister in this area. Lift up to God any concerns or questions that you have. Trust that he is listening and will guide you.

— Day 4 —

No Longer an Outsider

The first thing we learn about Ruth is that she was a Moabite (see Ruth 1:4). The Bible continues to describe her in that way throughout the story: "Ruth the Moabite" (Ruth 1:22; 2:2, 21; 4:5, 10). This detail can be easily overlooked in our modern-day culture. But to the ancient Israelite audience, Ruth's ethnicity would have been a big deal.

The reputation of Moabite women among the Jewish people wasn't good. When the Israelites were crossing the Jordan River under Joshua's leadership, "the men began to indulge in sexual immorality with Moabite women, who invited them to the sacrifices to their gods. The people ate the sacrificial meal and bowed down before these gods. So Israel yoked themselves to the Baal of Peor. And the LORD's anger burned against them" (Numbers 25:1–3).

Because of this, a law regarding the Moabites was put in place: "No Ammonite or Moabite or any of their descendants may enter the assembly of the LORD, not even in the tenth generation" (Deuteronomy 23:3). So, Ruth entering the gates of Bethlehem as a Moabite would have caused a stir. The fact that Naomi was willing to be seen with her is a testament to her character. The fact Boaz was willing to marry her is an equal testament to his character.

Outsiders are not always treated kindly in our society. You likely have firsthand experience with this, either as the outsider yourself or someone who has seen them being judged. We approach those who are different—whether they differ in gender, race, ethnicity, or social class—with suspicion. We are not always quick to welcome or accept outsiders.

Naomi and Boaz could have rejected Ruth as an outsider. Instead, they both embraced her. They made her their family. Because of this, Ruth became central to the story of Jesus. As the great-grandmother of King David, she was actually a direct descendent of Jesus.

At Pentecost, the Holy Spirit was poured out on the believers (see Acts 2). It is worth noting that in this moment, as prophesied by the prophet Joel, all boundary lines and barriers were erased: gender, age, and socioeconomic status. In Christ, everyone finds their place to belong, even the "outsiders." What a wonderful God we have!

Read | Ruth 2:4–12 and Galatians 3:26–28

Reflect

1. When Boaz first spotted Ruth in his field, he asked an overseer who she was. The overseer immediately identified Ruth as a Moabite who came back from Moab with Naomi. But instead of judging Ruth, Boaz showed kindness to her, assuring her that she would be under his protection. Ruth seemed surprised by his response. What did she call herself in verse 10? How do you think she expected Boaz to treat her?

2. Boaz responded by calling out all the things that he had heard about Ruth—that she left her homeland and everything she knew to help her mother-in-law. How does this reveal the way in which Boaz viewed Ruth?

3. According to Galatians 3:26–28, how does God see those who choose to put their faith in Jesus? What does this tell you about the inclusive nature of the gospel?

4. Paul wrote, "So in Christ Jesus you are all children of God through faith" (verse 26). What does it mean to you to be a part of God's own family? Why do you never have to be on the "outside" when it comes to your relationship with God?

Pray | If you resonate with Ruth the Moabite and feel like an outsider today—whether that is in your community, family, church, or elsewhere—bring that before the Lord. Ask him to comfort you and remind you that in him, you are embraced and accepted. If you feel convicted for having judged an outsider, bring that before the Lord as well. What is he telling you about this person? What is he revealing in your own heart that you can explore?

Day 5

Life with God

If you have been journeying with God for any length of time, you know to expect the unexpected. Your circumstances can go from dire to divine, from sorrowful to joyful, from unclear to certain—all seemingly overnight—when you are following God. You may not understand what he is doing in the moment, but when you look back at your life, what do you see? The hand of God at work.

Just think about Naomi's life. Her journey was unexpected on all accounts. An Israelite, she moves from Bethlehem to the land of Moab to escape a famine. While in this foreign land, her husband dies. Her sons marry two Moabite women, and then those sons also die. Naomi travels back to her homeland with a Moabite daughter-in-law. Destitute and penniless, the women enter into Bethlehem's gates. Naomi even tells her old friends to call her Mara, which means "bitter," "because the Almighty has made my life very bitter" (Ruth 1:20).

Once in Bethlehem, Ruth begins gleaning to support her and Naomi and happens upon the field of Boaz, one of Naomi's kinsman-redeemers. Boaz notices Ruth before he even knows who she is. He ultimately takes Ruth and Naomi under his protection. By the end of the book, Naomi is once again going by the name Naomi, which means "pleasant," and is being praised by her friends for her good fortune: "Praise be to the LORD, who this day has not left you without a guardian-redeemer. May he become famous throughout Israel! He will renew your life and sustain you in your old age. For your daughter-in-law, who loves you and who is better to you than seven sons, has given him birth" (4:14–15).

Maybe your life has similar twists and turns. Maybe you have also gone by another name—one that reflects where you felt you were in life: *bitter, destitute, unsure of the future before you*. And maybe you experienced God's redemption in a powerful and unexpected way. Or maybe you're still waiting on God, hoping that he will turn your story around, just as he did with Naomi's. If we can learn anything from this widow's story, it is that God is never done with us. He always has a plan, and that plan is better than anything we could imagine.

Read | Jeremiah 29:11–14

Reflect

1. The prophet Jeremiah was active in Judah from the thirteenth year of King Josiah until the fall of Jerusalem at the hands of the Babylonians (c. 626–587 BC). He was instructed by God to warn the people about their impending capture, which was a hard truth for them to hear. But Jeremiah also prophesied that God would not forget them in captivity and would deliver them. According to this passage, what were God's plans for his people? What did God say would happen when his people sought after him?

2. Based on this passage, how would you describe God's relationship with Israel?

3. If you drew out your own life's timeline, what would it look like? What ups and downs have you faced? When has the unexpected happened?

4. When you consider your life, where do you see God's hand at work? Is there evidence that his plan is to prosper you and give you hope and a future? Explain your response.

Pray | Reflect on today's passage during your prayer time. Read it as if the words are just for you—as if your good Father is telling you that he has a plan, a purpose, a hope, and a future for you. Trust in his promise that you will find him when you seek him.

For Next Week

Before you meet again with your group, read pages 144–151 in chapter 10 of *The God of the Way*. Also go back and complete any of the study and reflection questions from this personal study that you weren't able to finish.

WEEK 4

BEFORE GROUP MEETING	Read pages 144–151 in chapter 10 of *The God of the Way* Read the Welcome section (page 81)
GROUP MEETING	Discuss the Connect questions Watch the video teaching for session 4 Discuss the questions that follow as a group Do the closing exercise and pray (pages 81–92)
PERSONAL STUDY – DAY 1	Complete the daily study (pages 94–95)
PERSONAL STUDY – DAY 2	Complete the daily study (pages 96–97)
PERSONAL STUDY – DAY 3	Complete the daily study (pages 98–99)
PERSONAL STUDY – DAY 4	Complete the daily study (pages 100–101)
PERSONAL STUDY – DAY 5 (before week 5 group meeting)	Complete the daily study (pages 102–103) Read chapter 11 in *The God of the Way* Complete any unfinished personal studies

Boaz

GOD REDEEMS OUR LIVES

Then Boaz announced to the elders and all the people, "Today you are witnesses that I have bought from Naomi all the property of Elimelek, Kilion and Mahlon. I have also acquired Ruth the Moabite, Mahlon's widow, as my wife, in order to maintain the name of the dead with his property, so that his name will not disappear from among his family or from his hometown. Today you are witnesses!"

RUTH 4:9–10

Israel Under the Judges

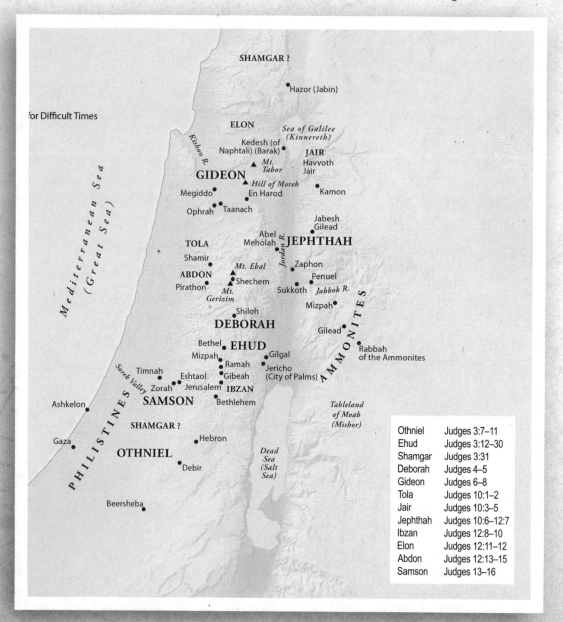

SHAMGAR ?

Hazor (Jabin)

for Difficult Times

ELON

Sea of Galilee (Kinnereth)

Kedesh (of Naphtali) (Barak)

JAIR

Kishon R.

▲ *Mt. Tabor*

GIDEON

Havvoth Jair

▲ *Hill of Moreh*

En Harod

Kamon

Megiddo

Mediterranean Sea (Great Sea)

Ophrah   Taanach

Jabesh Gilead

Abel Meholah

Jordan R.

JEPHTHAH

TOLA

Shamir

Zaphon

ABDON   *Mt. Ebal* ▲

Pirathon   Shechem

Penuel

Mt. Gerizim

Sukkoth   *Jabbok R.*

Shiloh

Mizpah

DEBORAH

Gilead

Bethel   EHUD

AMMONITES

Mizpah   Gilgal

Rabbah of the Ammonites

Timnah   Ramah

Sorek Valley   Eshtaol   Jericho (City of Palms)

Zorah   Gibeah

Jerusalem   IBZAN

SAMSON   Bethlehem

Ashkelon

PHILISTINES

Tableland of Moab (Mishor)

SHAMGAR ?

Gaza   Hebron

OTHNIEL

Debir   *Dead Sea (Salt Sea)*

Beersheba

Othniel	Judges 3:7–11
Ehud	Judges 3:12–30
Shamgar	Judges 3:31
Deborah	Judges 4–5
Gideon	Judges 6–8
Tola	Judges 10:1–2
Jair	Judges 10:3–5
Jephthah	Judges 10:6–12:7
Ibzan	Judges 12:8–10
Elon	Judges 12:11–12
Abdon	Judges 12:13–15
Samson	Judges 13–16

Welcome | Read On Your Own

In the last session, you looked at the story of Ruth and Naomi. Both of their husbands died while they were in Moab, so Naomi returned home to Bethlehem. She told Ruth to stay in Moab with her people, but Ruth refused, telling her mother-in-law that she would leave everything behind to follow her to Israel. Once there, God rewarded Ruth's faithfulness by bringing her into the fields of a landowner named Boaz. He showed great favor to Ruth—to the extent that he told the workers in his field to leave grain for her to glean.

There are people like Boaz in our world today. Maybe you've run into this type of person. You're at the grocery store, and you realize you forgot your wallet. The stranger behind you offers to pay. You're a college student, and you miss your final exam due to traffic. The professor lets you take it the next day. You fall ill, and you can't afford treatment. Someone hears about you, starts a fundraiser, and within a week you have everything you need. These type of everyday saviors sweep in to rescue the day. They redeem a lost situation.

In Jewish tradition, this person was called a kinsman-redeemer. By law, the kinsman-redeemer could save someone from financial ruin by taking that person under his wing and making him or her a part of his family. Ruth and Naomi desperately needed this type of protection . . . and so do we. Maybe we aren't destitute or suffering at the hands of a patriarchal society like Ruth and Naomi were, but we all need redemption. We all need people who can vouch for us, protect us, and put us under the safety of their wing.

What Boaz did for Ruth, Jesus did for us. The story of Ruth and Boaz is part of a great story that runs throughout Scripture—a story that points to Jesus.

Connect | 15 minutes

Welcome to session 4 of *The God Who Sees*. To get things started for this week's group time, discuss one of the following questions:

- What is a key insight or takeaway from last week's personal study that you would like to share with the group?

— *or* —

- When is a time that you desperately needed help and a modern-day "Boaz" came through for you? What did that person do for you?

Watch | 20 minutes

Now watch the video for this session. As you watch, use the following outline to record any thoughts or concepts that stand out to you.

I. What was the purpose of the kinsman-redeemer in Israel in Ruth and Naomi's day?

    A. It was impossible in ancient Israel for women to survive without a male relative.

        1. In that day—in that patriarchal society—women were not allowed to own land.

        2. If the husband of a woman died, she could receive land from him, but she was not allowed to keep it. She needed a male relative for the land to stay in the family.

        3. When a woman was widowed, none of the provisions that a husband left her could belong to her. If she had a son, that male child would be the one to provide for her.

    B. In the patriarchal culture in which Ruth and Naomi lived, it was only the males in the family who could earn money, trade, and conduct business. It was the men who held all the rights.

        1. Given this, the law established that a male relative, known as a *kinsman-redeemer*, could intervene into the widow's situation, take her for his wife, and provide for her.

        2. In assuming this role, the kinsman-redeemer also took control of the widow's possessions, as he was the only one allowed to do transactional business on her behalf.

The City Gate

By the end of the fourth century BC, defensive walls were a regular feature of cities found in Mesopotamia, the fertile region between the Tigris and Euphrates rivers where ancient cultures flourished (modern-day Syria, Iraq, and Kuwait).[28] In the Bible, the first mention of a walled city is found in the story of God's judgment against Sodom in Genesis 19:1–29. This indicates the cities in Canaan likely had defensive walls by c. 2000–1900 BC, the date that many scholars and archeologists believe the destruction of Sodom and Gomorrah took place.[29]

Of course, the fact that cities had walls meant that a way was needed for people to enter and leave. Under normal conditions, this access was given through *posterns*, which were narrow entrances in or beneath the walls that could be easily blocked during an attack. But for commerce and everyday life to take place, larger entrances were needed so that animal herds, transport vehicles, royal and religious processions, and large groups of people and troops could easily move in and out. City planners accomplished this by creating fortified city gates.[30]

Over time, these gates became more than just access points. Merchants were forced to use them to bring their goods in and out of a city, so the gates became places where people would congregate to see what new wares had arrived. This activity, in turn, led to the gates becoming a sort of civic forum where city elders oversaw legal procedures, traders swapped stories and goods, kings and officials sat to take counsel, and everyone else who wanted to be seen and heard by the city's population gathered to proclaim their messages.[31]

Given this, it is little wonder that when Boaz wanted to conduct the business of becoming Ruth and Naomi's kinsman-redeemer, he headed straight to the city gate. Boaz knew that if he waited there long enough, the closer relative with whom he wanted to meet would show up. Boaz also knew that when the man did arrive, the elders of the town would be there to serve as witnesses and proclaim the arrangement was legal and in order (see Ruth 4:1–12).

3. The law in Israel was specific as to which male relative in the widow's family was given first priority in choosing to become her kinsman-redeemer.

C. The rules regarding the kinsman-redeemer were established in the law of Moses.

  1. In Leviticus 25:25–27, we read that if an Israelite male became so poor that he had to sell some of his land to survive, his nearest male relative could buy back that land.

  2. This nearest relative (or "kinsman") of the man was thus allowed to "redeem" the family's land by doing business on behalf of his poorer relative.

  3. In Genesis 38:8, we see this law being applied in the case of a woman whose husband had died. The husband's brother was given this instruction: "Sleep with your brother's wife and fulfill your duty to her as a brother-in-law to raise up offspring for your brother."

II. How did Boaz step into the role of becoming Ruth and Naomi's kinsman-redeemer?

A. Ruth was actually not eligible to have a kinsman-redeemer because she was from Moab.

  1. In Ruth 2:10, we read that Ruth said the following to Boaz: "Why have I found such favor in your eyes that you notice me—a foreigner?" Ruth was acknowledging that she did not deserve the favor that Boaz was showing to her because she was an outsider.

  2. In fact, Ruth was only eligible to marry another man who could serve as the family's kinsman-redeemer because of *Naomi*. Ruth had married into her family's bloodline.

  3. Ruth also needed Naomi because, again, as a foreigner, she would not have known how to secure a kinsman-redeemer. Naomi understood the customs in Israel.

B. Naomi proved to be the grand master in instructing Ruth on how to let Boaz know that she wanted him to marry her and serve as the family's kinsman-redeemer (see Ruth 3:1–11).

1. Boaz indicated that he wanted to do as Ruth had asked, but there was another family member who was closer in line. He told Ruth that he would meet with this man and at least ask if he wanted to fulfill this role (see Ruth 3:12–13).

2. The next day, Boaz went into the town and sat down at the city gates (see Ruth 4:1). Everyone passed through the gates, so it was the ideal place for the men of the town to be seen and meet with each other to conduct business transactions.

3. The fact that Boaz did this is a testament to his character. At the end of the day, we don't know if this closer relative even knew that Ruth or Naomi existed before this conversation with Boaz.

C. Boaz, being an honorable man, meets with the male relative and tells him it is actually his place to take the position of Ruth and Naomi's kinsman-redeemer (see Ruth 4:2–4).

1. The relative at first agrees to redeem the land. But after hearing it would require him to marry Ruth, he declines because it could endanger his own estate (see Ruth 4:5–6).

2. So Boaz agrees to fulfill the role of kinsman-redeemer. He and the relative conduct a ceremony to show that the transfer of the property has been made. The action is done before witnesses, who affirm a legal transaction has been made (see Ruth 4:7–12).

3. Boaz is a foreshadowing of Jesus, for the role of the kinsman-redeemer is symbolic of our Lord's mediating work. Jesus is the kinsman-redeemer for all humankind.

III. What do we learn from the story about the importance of kindness in God's family?

    A. What precedes this event is an act of kindness that Boaz showed to Ruth when he told his workers to purposefully leave grain in the fields for her to glean (see Ruth 2:15–16).

        1. Boaz abundantly provided for Ruth, just as God abundantly provides for us.

        2. As Jesus said, "The thief does not come except to steal, and to kill, and to destroy. I have come that they may have life, and that they may have it more abundantly" (John 10:10 NKJV).

        3. The word for *life* used in this is *zoe*, and it means "life beyond containment." The life that God has for us is so huge and overflowing that it cannot be contained.

    B. Boaz extended *hesed* (loving-kindness) toward Ruth. When she asked why he was showing her favor, he responded with a statement that shows her character: "I've been told all about what you have done for your mother-in-law" (Ruth 2:11).

        1. Boaz and Ruth were kind to each other but also to everyone around them.

        2. God had a plan for them all along. We often can't see the tapestry that God is weaving in our lives. We can't understand his ways because they are not our ways. He does not think the way we think. But ultimately, he has only good plans in store for us.

        3. As Paul writes, "[God] chose us in Him before the foundation of the world, that we should be holy and without blame before Him in love" (Ephesians 1:4 NKJV).

Shoes in Boaz's Day

"Now in earlier times in Israel, for the redemption and transfer of property to become final, one party took off his sandal and gave it to the other. This was the method of legalizing transactions in Israel" (Ruth 4:7). It is difficult to determine exactly when humans first began wearing shoes. Scholars believe—based on changes in foot shape and toe strength seen in bones recovered from archaeological digs—that people might have begun wearing them some 40,000 years ago.[32] Shoes were certainly common enough in biblical times for them to play a role in Israelite society, as is seen in the interaction between Boaz and his relative in the book of Ruth.

The Bible reveals that the act of removing one's shoes was a sign of reverence, humility, and respect. When God called Moses to lead the Israelites, he appeared in the form of a burning bush. When Moses went over to investigate, God said to him, "Do not come any closer. . . . Take off your sandals, for the place where you are standing is holy ground" (Exodus 3:5). The ground where the bush was burning—where sheep and goats traversed—was not holy in and of itself. Rather, it was "holy ground" because the presence of God was there. For this reason, Moses needed to show proper respect of God's presence by removing his shoes. God would later instruct Joshua in much the same way (see Joshua 5:13–15).

Shoes also served a symbolic function in a Jewish custom known as *halizah*. As we have seen, the law of Moses mandated that when a married man died without an heir, and had an unmarried brother, that brother was obligated to marry his widow (see Deuteronomy 25:5–6). However, that relative could release the widow to marry someone else through the ceremony of *halizah*. The brother-in-law would wear a special shoe on his right foot made of a kosher animal that did not contain any metal. The widow would declare that her brother-in-law refused to marry her, place her left hand on his calf, untie the laces with her right hand, throw the shoe to the ground, and spit on the ground in front of him (see verses 7–10).

The shoe served as the symbol of the transaction and that the brother-in-law had released his obligations.[33]

C. When you look at the bloodline of Boaz and Ruth, they couldn't have imagined how God would use them. The same is true in our stories. We never know how God will use us.

    1. Ruth and Boaz were married and had a son named Obed. Obed had a son named Jesse. Jesse got married and had a son named David (see Ruth 4:21–22).

    2. David, the "runt" of the litter, became the king over all Israel. Generations later in his bloodline, a man named Joseph was born and took Mary as his wife. She became pregnant through the Holy Spirit and gave birth to Jesus (see Matthew 1:5–16).

    3. Jesus came from the line of David to fulfill prophecies of old (see Isaiah 11:1–16).

IV. What is the significance of the threshing floor in Boaz and Ruth's story?

    A. The threshing floor was where the harvest was prepared by separating the grain from the straw. It was here that Ruth asked Boaz to spread the corner of his garment over her (in other words, to protect her) and to serve as the family's kinsman-redeemer.

        1. The Bible states, "Solomon began to build the temple of the LORD in Jerusalem on Mount Moriah, where the LORD had appeared to his father David. It was on the threshing floor of Araunah the Jebusite, the place provided by David" (2 Chronicles 3:1).

        2. The location of the threshing floor where Solomon built the temple is the same location where Abraham took Isaac to offer him as a sacrifice (see Genesis 22:1–19).

        3. It is not known if the threshing floor in Boaz's field is the same as that of Araunah. But we see that the threshing floor represents a place *where redemption happens.*

B. David acquired the threshing floor of Araunah after he took a census of the people to prove the strength of his army (see 1 Chronicles 21:1). This was forbidden by God, because the Lord wanted his people to rely totally on him and not on the strength of an army.

    1. David realizes he has sinned and repents before God. But God makes David endure a punishment. The Lord allows one-third of David's army to die (see 1 Chronicles 21:8–14).

    2. David goes to buy the threshing floor of a man named Araunah. Araunah wants to give it to him, but David says, "No, I insist on paying the full price. I will not take for the LORD what is yours, or sacrifice a burnt offering that costs me nothing" (1 Chronicles 21:24).

    3. So we see that just as redemption happened on the threshing floor in Boaz and Ruth's story, redemption happens on the threshing floor in King David's story.

C. The threshing floor is a place of *crushing grain.* It is in this place of crushing grain that redemption takes place. Jesus was also crushed so that we could be redeemed.

    1. Right in the middle of the temple that Solomon built was the holy of holies. This was the most sacred place where God's presence resided. Only the high priests could enter this room, which happened only one time each year on the Day of Atonement.

    2. On the Day of Atonement, the high priest sacrificed a lamb to atone for the sins of everyone. Regardless of the conflict that occurs today at this place where the temple once stood, it is a place of redemption because Jesus is the ultimate kinsman-redeemer.

    3. What Boaz did for Ruth is the ultimate depiction of what Jesus did for us. He covered us. He made us his bride. He has provided everything for us.

Discuss | 35 minutes

Take some time to discuss what you just watched by answering the following questions. There are some suggested questions below to help you begin your discussion, but feel free to pick any of the additional questions as time allows.

Suggested Questions

1. In the patriarchal society of Ruth and Naomi's day, women were not allowed to own property in Israel. This meant that when a woman's husband died, she was not allowed to keep the land. What system was established to allow a woman to keep her family's land? How did this law apply in Ruth and Naomi's situation?

2. Ruth was not eligible to have a kinsman-redeemer because she was considered a foreigner (from the land of Moab). However, what did allow her to have a kinsman-redeemer? How did Naomi help Ruth to secure Boaz's protection over them?

3. In Ephesians 4:32, the apostle Paul wrote, "Be kind and compassionate to one another, forgiving each other, just as in Christ God forgave you." How did Boaz demonstrate loving-kindness to Ruth? How did Ruth demonstrate loving-kindness to Naomi?

4. The place where Naomi instructed Ruth to lie down and uncover Boaz's feet was a threshing floor. What is the significance of the threshing floor in Scripture?

Additional Questions

5. Read Leviticus 25:25–27. This law stated what the Israelites were to do if a *male* member of society became so poor that he had to sell some of his property. In what ways did this law allow a family to potentially retain their land?

6. Boaz was an honorable man, so when Ruth asked him to be her kinsman-redeemer, he had to inform her, "Although it is true that I am a guardian-redeemer of our family, there is another who is more closely related than I" (Ruth 3:12). What steps did Boaz take the next day to approach this family member? What was the result?

7. One of the surprises in Boaz and Ruth's story is that David (the king of Israel) came from their bloodline, as did Jesus (the King of kings). God used Boaz and Ruth in his plans, even though she was considered an "outsider." What does this say about how God uses people today—regardless of their background or family history?

8. As you consider the role that Boaz played in Ruth and Naomi's story, what parallels do you see between him as their kinsman-redeemer and Jesus as the ultimate kinsman-redeemer? How is what Boaz did for Ruth a depiction of what Jesus did for us?

Respond | 10 minutes

Review the outline for the video teaching and any notes you took. In the space below, write down your most significant takeaway from this session.

Pray | 10 minutes

End your time by praying as a group, thanking Jesus that he is your ultimate kinsman-redeemer. Ask if anyone has any prayer requests to share. Write those requests down in the space below so you and your group members can pray about them in the week ahead.

Name   Request

Personal Study

As you discussed this week, God desires for us to show kindness to one another (see Ephesians 4:32). Boaz demonstrated his kindness to Ruth by leaving extra grain in his fields, by inviting her to share a meal with him, and ultimately by agreeing to become her and Naomi's kinsman-redeemer. Boaz's acts of kindness point us to Jesus, who performed the ultimate act of kindness and love by offering us redemption and salvation. As you explore these themes this week, be sure to write down your responses to the questions in the spaces provided, as you will be given a few minutes to share your insights at the start of the next session. If you are reading *The God of the Way* alongside this study, first review pages 144–151 in chapter 10 of the book.

– Day 1 –

The *Goel* as Redeemer

Ruth and Naomi arrived in Bethlehem in a vulnerable state. As widows, they were essentially destitute without the provision of a male. They could not own property and had no inheritance rights. Women in most modern societies marry by choice, not because they need a man to protect them. However, the culture of Ruth and Naomi's day made it incredibly difficult for them to survive without a man. Their economic stability and social status depended on it.

Ruth soon went to work in a field where she could glean grain from the harvesters, picking up whatever they happened to drop as they went about their work. What she didn't know was that the field was owned by a man named Boaz. Ruth didn't know who he was, but he noticed her and felt protective of her.

When Ruth later told Naomi whose field she gleaned—and showed her the large bundle of grain that she had gleaned—Naomi exclaimed, "'May he be blessed by the LORD, who has not forsaken his kindness to the living or the dead.' Naomi continued, 'The man is a close relative. He is one of our family redeemers'" (Ruth 2:20 HCSB).

A family redeemer, also called a kinsman-redeemer, is known as a *goel* in the Hebrew language. According to Jewish tradition, a *goel* was someone who could step in and intervene for a family in trouble. If a man was in debt and had to sell his land, the *goel* could buy that land to keep it in the family (see Leviticus 25). In the case of Ruth and Naomi, this meant that Boaz could buy back whatever land Naomi's husband, Elimelech, had sold when he and Naomi moved to Moab.

This type of provision could only be divine and points us to the greater and better Boaz: Jesus, the Messiah. He is our *goel*. When we were lost and destitute, he came to redeem us, to buy us back from the sin to which we were enslaved, and to set us free. Jesus extends to us the same love and protection that Boaz extended to Ruth and Naomi. He is our one and only redeemer.

Read | Ruth 4:9–15 and Ephesians 1:5–8

Reflect

1. Boaz announced to a group of elders, who served as witnesses, that he was becoming Ruth and Naomi's family redeemer. Boaz married Ruth, and the couple had a son. What did the women of the town say to Naomi when they learned that Ruth had given birth to a son? What does this tell us about the importance of a family redeemer?

2. According to the apostle Paul in Ephesians 1:5–8, what status do we have with God through Jesus? How did Jesus give us this status? How is our redemption through Christ similar to Ruth and Naomi's redemption through Boaz?

3. When is a time that you were able to intervene on someone's behalf, saving that person from a dire situation? What were you able to do for that individual?

4. When did you first become aware of Jesus as your redeemer? How do you need his redemption today? (Or, if you haven't yet had a moment like this, how has this study made you think differently about Jesus' role in your life as a redeemer?)

Pray | Spend your prayer time talking to Jesus, your *goel*. Thank him for saving you from sin. Praise him for being your redeemer. Ask him to continue his work of redemption in your life.

- Day 2 -

The *Goel* as Protector

Growing up, did you have a big brother who looked out for you? A friend who had your back? A parent who you knew would protect you no matter what? Knowing we have someone in our corner is comforting, especially when we are in a new place. This is what Ruth had in Boaz. As a foreigner, and especially as a widow, she needed a protector, someone to look out for her.

Boaz noticed Ruth's vulnerability. He noticed that she was a new worker in his field, that she was a foreigner, and that she was unmarried. Without knowing who she was—or that he would soon marry her—he ordered the young male workers not to touch her. He told Ruth how to stay safe while working what could be a risky job for a woman of her status (see Ruth 2:8-9). How comforting this must have felt for Ruth to have someone looking out for her when all of her protections—her husband, her father-in-law, her Moabite family—were gone.

The world can often feel like a cruel and lonely place. Maybe you had someone in your life who looked out for you when you were younger, but no one is looking out for you now. Maybe you feel like you have to fend for yourself, with no spouse, friends, or community around you for support. But just like Ruth had a protector in Boaz, so you have a protector in Jesus. He is the author and defender of your faith, the Son of God, and your Great High Priest. He is there when we need him the most. He is there when you are feeling vulnerable. He is there when it seems like nobody else is. Jesus is your protector.

Read | John 17:11–23

Reflect

1. In this passage from the Gospel of John, we see Jesus praying for us, and we see him praying for his disciples. As he was preparing to leave them, he left them his Spirit

and his protection—the same Spirit and protection that we have today. What did Jesus pray for his disciples? What did Jesus pray for us?

2. According to Jesus' prayer, how are we protected? According to verse 23, how will the world know that God sent his Son?

3. How have you felt God's protection over your life? How have you witnessed God's protection in the lives of your friends and loved ones?

4. What type of protection do you need today—spiritually, physically, or emotionally?

Pray | Bring any fears or anxieties before your heavenly Father. Ask him to protect you by the power of his name and his word. Ask Jesus to intercede on your behalf. Believe that the same protection that Jesus left for his disciples . . . he has also left for you.

- Day 3 -

The Threshing Floor

Boaz and Ruth's story culminated in the events that happened during the night on what is called a threshing floor. As mentioned in this week's teaching, the threshing floor is where the grain harvest was winnowed—a process where the workers tossed the grain into the air with a fork, allowing the wind to carry off the chaff (a part of the grain that couldn't be used) and the heavier grain to fall to the ground, where it was collected.

Each night during the harvest season, someone would sleep on the threshing floor to prevent thieves or animals from taking the grain.[34] The night Ruth visited Boaz, it was his turn to guard the grain. Separating the wheat from the chaff is a metaphor used elsewhere in Scripture to represent the separation of God's true people from those who are not. The same metaphor could be at play here with Boaz. On the threshing floor, we see his character tested, and as you will read in today's passage, we find he is a man loyal to God and the law.

Boaz, instead of taking advantage of Ruth, gave her his protection. Instead of shaming her, he honored her request and told her how to preserve her honor. Instead of taking a shortcut around the law, he upheld it. Boaz was tested—and passed with flying colors. This is not to say *Boaz* was perfect—rather, it was *God's* provision for Ruth and Naomi that was perfect. God brought them into the hands of a man who loved him and followed his ways. If there was any doubt in Ruth and Naomi's mind, the threshing floor reassured them.

Read | Ruth 2:7–15 and Luke 3:15–18

Reflect

1. How did Boaz react when he saw, in the dark of night, that there was a woman lying at his feet? How did Ruth identify herself, and what was her request to him?

2. How was Boaz's character tested on the threshing floor? What do we learn about his character from this interaction? How do you think Ruth felt after these events?

3. What did John the Baptist say to those who were wondering if he was the Messiah? What metaphors did he use to describe what the Messiah would do?

4. How has your character been tested on the metaphorical threshing floor? What did you learn about your strengths and weaknesses as you went through that situation?

Pray | Today, thank God for his perfect provision in your life through Jesus. Praise him that even when your character is lacking, you can know that in your weakness, he is strong.

-Day 4-

The Road of Obedience

God's calling is not always easy to follow. *You want me to go where? You want me to do what? You want me to reach out to who?* His ways are higher than your ways (see Isaiah 55:9), so his plans may not always make sense to you or sound fun. (Quite the opposite, in fact.) But no matter where God leads, the road of obedience is always rewarded.

In Boaz's case, his obedience led him to be written down in history. We don't see any of his questions recorded in Scripture, but we can guess—based on our own experiences with God's calling—that he might have wondered about a few things. *God, should I really marry Naomi's daughter-in-law? She is a foreigner from enemy territory. What will the people think if I do this? Should I really take on this task of becoming her and Naomi's kinsman-redeemer?*

While Boaz had his questions, he ultimately decided on the path of obedience. We saw in this week's teaching where it led him: "Boaz [was] the father of Obed, Obed the father of Jesse, and Jesse the father of David" (Ruth 4:21–22). Boaz's obedience not only led him to a loyal and faithful wife like Ruth but it also put him in Jesus' bloodline.

Sometimes our reward for obedience is something external, like Boaz being rememberd in Scripture and his line going down in history. But often our obedience leads to internal rewards like peace, joy, contentment, and deep faith. Regardless, no matter where our obedience leads us, we can trust that when we are saying yes to God, we are going in the right direction. The road of obedience will not lead us astray.

Read | Matthew 22:34–40 and 2 John 1:1–6

Reflect

1. The Pharisees tested Jesus to see how well this rabbi from Nazareth knew the law. Jesus quoted directly from Mosaic law (Deuteronomy and Leviticus). How would you summarize the two greatest laws we are called to follow? What do you think

the Pharisees thought of Jesus' reply? What does this passage tell you about what obedience to Jesus looks like?

2. The apostle John addressed his second epistle to a "dear lady," which either refers to a congregation or the woman who hosted the congregation.[35] In the early days of Christianity, there was a lot of confusion about who Jesus was and what this new religion was. It was important that believers accurately represented Jesus and what he was about. How did John echo what Jesus told the Pharisees? Why was it important for Jesus' early followers to display this type of love—and why is it important today?

3. Think about a time you followed the path of obedience toward God. What did you do and what was the experience like? Did you reap any external or internal rewards?

4. What do you feel God calling you to be obedient in today? This could be something big or small. How do you feel about the idea of being obedient in this area of your life?

Pray | Spend some time praying about where you sense God is leading you today. Ask him to give you the faith of Boaz and the grace of Jesus. Whatever is holding you back from taking that step of obedience, bring it to the Father, knowing you will be met with love and kindness.

— Day 5 —

The House of Bread

When we're hungry, we eat. When we're thirsty, we drink. When we're tired, we sleep. We know what is needed to meet our basic physical needs. But what about our emotional, relational, and spiritual needs? The truth is that we often don't go to our heavenly Father to meet those needs. Rather, we go to alternative sources: money, power, popularity, and the like.

You may have noticed that *grain* is a recurring image in the story of Ruth and Boaz. Boaz owns a wheat field. Ruth gleans grain from that field. They decide to marry on the threshing floor of that field. Boaz seals this promise with grain to bring back to Naomi.

Grain, as we know, is used to make *bread*. Perhaps to underline this theme, the translation of the Hebrew name for Bethlehem—where Boaz's field was located and all of these events took place—is "house of bread."[36] When Ruth was desperate and downtrodden, she went straight to the source of her provision: the house of bread. Boaz provided Ruth with grain and became her and Naomi's ultimate provider as their family redeemer.

When we turn to the New Testament, we find that Jesus also had a thing or two to say about bread. He called himself the "bread of life"—the spiritual source of everything we need (John 6:35). While Boaz represented a portion of God's provision, Jesus embodied God's full provision—forgiveness of our sins and an eternity with God. So, where are you going to meet your emotional, relational, and spiritual needs? Consider going to the one and only source that can truly meet those needs—Jesus, your Boaz, the Bread of Life.

Read | John 6:30–40

Reflect

1. Shortly before Jesus had this exchange, he had performed the miracle of multiplying bread and fish to feed a crowd of 5,000 (see John 6:1–15). Yet the people wanted to see more signs so they could be certain who Jesus was. They requested a sign like the one

God sent to Moses and the Israelites while they wandered in the desert. God provided manna (a sweet bread) for them to eat each day (see Exodus 16). How did Jesus respond to their request? What did he mean by describing himself as the "bread of life"?

2. Jesus told the crowd, "As I told you, you have seen me and still you do not believe" (verse 36). Jesus knew that regardless of the signs he performed, there would still be those who doubted that he was the Messiah. What does Jesus say in verses 37–40 about those who took the leap of faith and chose to believe in him?

3. Jesus promised, "I am the bread of life. Whoever comes to me will never go hungry, and whoever believes in me will never be thirsty" (verse 35). How have you experienced Jesus as your Bread of Life? How has he satisfied your spiritual hunger and thirst?

4. What emotional, relational, or spiritual needs do you need the Bread of Life to provide for you? What will you do to bring those needs before him?

Pray | Come to the Bread of Life today and tell Jesus what you need. Trust that he has everything to meet that need. If you've been going elsewhere in search of provision, also talk to Jesus about this. Ask him to help you believe that he is the source of all you need.

For Next Week

Before you meet again with your group, read chapter 11 of *The God of the Way*. Also go back and complete any of the study and reflection questions from this personal study that you weren't able to finish.

WEEK 5

BEFORE GROUP MEETING	Read chapter 11 in *The God of the Way* Read the Welcome section (page 107)
GROUP MEETING	Discuss the Connect questions Watch the video teaching for session 5 Discuss the questions that follow as a group Do the closing exercise and pray (pages 107–118)
PERSONAL STUDY – DAY 1	Complete the daily study (pages 120–121)
PERSONAL STUDY – DAY 2	Complete the daily study (pages 122–123)
PERSONAL STUDY – DAY 3	Complete the daily study (pages 124–125)
PERSONAL STUDY – DAY 4	Complete the daily study (pages 126–127)
PERSONAL STUDY – DAY 5 (before week 6 group meeting)	Complete the daily study (pages 128–129) Read chapter 12 in *The God of the Way* Complete any unfinished personal studies

David

GOD NEVER OVERLOOKS US

Jesse had seven of his sons pass before Samuel, but Samuel said to him, "The LORD has not chosen these." So he asked Jesse, "Are these all the sons you have?" "There is still the youngest," Jesse answered. "He is tending the sheep." Samuel said, "Send for him; we will not sit down until he arrives." So he sent for him and had him brought in.

1 SAMUEL 16:10–12

The Kingdom of Israel

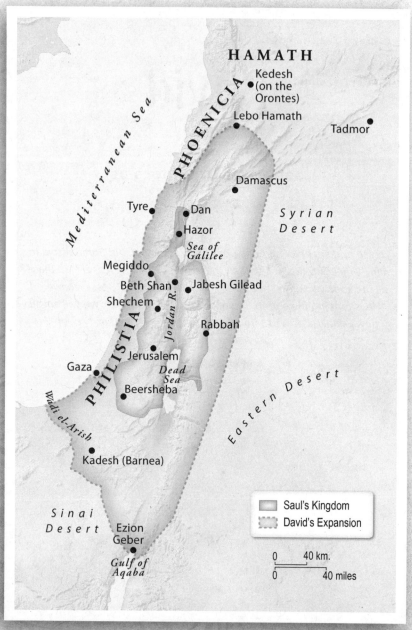

HAMATH

Kedesh (on the Orontes)

Lebo Hamath

Tadmor

Mediterranean Sea

PHOENICIA

Damascus

Tyre

Dan

Hazor

Sea of Galilee

Syrian Desert

Megiddo

Beth Shan

Jabesh Gilead

Shechem

Jordan R.

PHILISTIA

Rabbah

Gaza

Jerusalem

Dead Sea

Beersheba

Eastern Desert

Wadi el-Arish

Kadesh (Barnea)

Sinai Desert

Ezion Geber

Gulf of Aqaba

Saul's Kingdom

David's Expansion

0   40 km.

0   40 miles

Welcome | Read On Your Own

In the last session, you concluded the story of Ruth and saw how God orchestrated events so that she ended up gleaning in the fields of a man named Boaz. When Boaz saw her, he showed favor to her, which ultimately led to Ruth's mother-in-law, Naomi, coming up with a scheme to secure Boaz as the family's kinsman-redeemer. Boaz was willing to take on the role and went through the necessary steps to make it happen.

But the story doesn't end there, because Ruth and Boaz's great-grandson was a man named David. David is an interesting character in the Bible because he was both a shepherd and a king. In a sense, he very much embodied both the lowly and the lofty. He knew what it was like to hold the humble position of shepherd, but he also knew the pressures of being king. He was "a man after [God's] own heart" (1 Samuel 13:14), yet he committed one of the greatest sins in Scripture. He was a strong leader but also could be a prideful man.

Despite David's complexities, he embodied what Jesus would embody generations later. Jesus also called himself a shepherd (see John 10:11), and he was a king (see John 18:36). He guided the people and led the people. But where David fell short, Jesus triumphed.

With Jesus as our shepherd, we can be confident that we are cared for and protected, and we can be confident that we have access to the Father. Jesus is our gateway—our only way. Other leaders may lead us astray, disappoint us, or hurt us. Political leaders, church leaders, thought leaders . . . they are all human in the end. But Jesus is the Good Shepherd who never lets us down, never leads us astray, and never hurts us. He leads us beside still waters, restores our souls, and guides us on paths of righteousness (see Psalm 23:2–3).

Connect | 15 minutes

Welcome to session 5 of *The God Who Sees*. To get things started for this week's group time, discuss one of the following questions:

- What is a key insight or takeaway from last week's personal study that you would like to share with the group?

— *or* —

- When is one time in your life that you knew God saw you in a dire situation? How did the Lord calm your fears during that troublesome time?

Watch | 20 minutes

Now watch the video for this session. As you watch, use the following outline to record any thoughts or concepts that stand out to you.

I. What does the Bible say about David and how he became the king of Israel?

A. There are quite a few people in the Bible who, because of the epic stories we read about them, are known by one name. This is certainly true of the man known simply as *David*.

1. David had humble beginnings, but he went on to become one of the most beloved characters in the Bible. His life teaches us so much about humility and surrender to God.

2. David, who authored many of the psalms, also teaches us about worship and how worshiping the Lord is sometimes countercultural and not accepted.

3. Even though David sinned, he was called in Scripture a man after God's own heart (see 1 Samuel 13:14).

B. David was the youngest of Jesse's sons. When the prophet Samuel came to anoint one of Jesse's sons to be the next king over Israel, he was out in the fields shepherding the sheep.

1. The prophet Samuel received a word from God to anoint one of Jesse's sons as the next king. Samuel didn't know which one he was supposed to anoint (see 1 Samuel 16:1–5).

2. So Jesse paraded each of his sons before Samuel, but each time the Lord said, "Nope, nope, nope." Finally, Samuel asked if Jesse had any other sons (see 1 Samuel 16:6–11).

3. Jesse told Samuel that his youngest, David, was out tending the sheep. He was brought in, and Samuel anointed him as king in front of his family (see 1 Samuel 16:12–13).

Shepherds in Israel

When we first encounter David, he is identified as a shepherd (see 1 Samuel 16:11). We learn that in this role, he has protected his father's flocks from lions and bears (17:34–35). So what would life have been like for David as a shepherd in his day?

In the ancient world, flocks were often mixed, with goats and sheep grazing together. The shepherd's life in many ways was quite simple, as it involved a lot of time just watching the animals graze. However, as noted in David's words to Saul, shepherding also involved certain hazards. Sheep were well suited to a nomadic existence, but they were not the brightest of creatures, and thus were very dependent on the shepherd for survival. The shepherd had to lead his flocks to grasslands where the sheep and goats could graze. He had to lead them to fresh water. He also had to protect them from predators like bears and lions.[37]

The garb of a shepherd typically consisted of a cotton tunic that was girded with a leather strap. Over this, the shepherd might wear an outer garment made of animal fur for warmth. He would carry a bag made of dried skin to store his food for the day—possibly bread, cheese, dried fruit, and olives. The shepherd carried a rod made of oak wood, generally with a knob at the end of it, to serve as a weapon against predators. He also carried a staff—a long stick that often had a crook at one end—to serve for walking in rough terrain and also to guide the sheep (see Psalm 23:4). The shepherd might also carry a sling, comprised of two strings with a leather receptable for the stone, to further protect and even guide the sheep.

The job of shepherd in an Israelite family usually fell to the youngest son. As a boy grew older and other sons arrived, he would transition into the role of helping his father sow, plow, and reap the family's crops, passing on the shepherding duties to the next youngest son in line. In this way, the job was passed from one son to the next, until the youngest of all became the family shepherd. So it is no surprise that David, the youngest of Jesse's sons, was out tending his father's flock as a shepherd and was not present when Samuel visited the home.[38]

C. There was a sequence of events that needed to occur in David's story for him to be anointed as king. The same is true in our lives—God uses a sequence of events to develop a warrior-heart within us.

    1. Sometimes, we don't like the way those events play out in our lives. David probably would not have picked the way God used to bring him to the throne of Israel.

    2. It would take many years from the time David was anointed by Samuel to actually become the king over Israel. There was not an immediate path for David's kingship.

    3. Further, during that time, David was often on the run for his life. This is because Saul was the reigning king, and he did not like the idea of giving up the throne.

II. What gave David the ability to endure all these trials on his way to becoming king?

A. David had already killed lions and bears as a shepherd (see 1 Samuel 17:34–35). He was a warrior, and this gave him the tenacity to come into this conflict with Saul.

    1. God orchestrated events so that early on, right after David was anointed, he came into the court of King Saul as a musician (see 1 Samuel 16:14–23).

    2. David, the man whom God had anointed king, was thus in the service of Saul, the man whom God had rejected as king. It must have been quite a conflict for David.

3. Saul eventually grew so jealous of David that he tried to kill him. Jonathan, Saul's son, was David's friend and stepped in to protect him (see 1 Samuel 18:10–11; 19:1–3).

B. The Bible relates that King Saul was suffering from an oppressive spirit.

1. Saul was continually unrepentant—continually doing what the enemy wanted him to do. So God's anointing and covering of protection was lifted from him (see 1 Samuel 16:14).

2. In the Old Testament, the Spirit of God would come on people and depart. We see how this happened in Saul's life. However, as New Testament believers, we have the assurance that Jesus paid the ransom of our sins for all time.

3. The anointing of God never leaves us now because of Jesus' sacrifice on the cross. The Bible is one continuous and beautiful love story of God for his creation.

C. One of the most beautiful things about David, as it relates to our own lives and experiences, is that he walked with God and saw his destiny fulfilled by God.

1. When we walk with God as David did, the Lord will fulfill the plans he has for our destiny. When we don't walk with God, as in Saul's case, our part in God's story isn't fulfilled.

2. Think of this in terms of a woven tapestry. Some of the threads are vibrant, while some are dull. The vibrant ones in this life are those who trust God and step out in faith.

3. Jesus said, "Seek first [God's] kingdom and his righteousness, and all these things will be given to you" (Matthew 6:33). David wasn't perfect, but he sought God first.

III. What is the significance of David being a shepherd before he became a king?

  A. David's life as a shepherd has parallels for us because Jesus is our Good Shepherd.

    1. Jesus said, "I am the gate; whoever enters through me will be saved" (John 10:9).

    2. In ancient Israel, there was no door for the sheep in a pen. The shepherd lay down in the opening. The sheep couldn't get out, and the predators couldn't get in.

    3. Jesus says he is the gate for the sheep. While the enemy, the thief, comes only to steal, kill, and destroy, the Good Shepherd comes to give us abundant life (see John 10:10).

  B. In the Old Testament, the Lord refers to the kings of Israel and Judah as shepherds (see, for example, Ezekiel 34:1–31). But these kings never had a heart for the sheep.

    1. Jesus, the Good Shepherd, actually lays down his life for the sheep (see John 10:15). This is amazing when you consider that sheep are not the brightest light bulbs in the box!

    2. The Bible says, "[The Good Shepherd] restores and revives my life. He opens before me the right path and leads me along in his footsteps of righteousness" (Psalm 23:3 TPT).

David's Waterfall

"After Saul returned from pursuing the Philistines, he was told, 'David is in the Desert of En Gedi.' So Saul took three thousand able young men from all Israel and set out to look for David and his men near the Crags of the Wild Goats" (1 Samuel 24:1–2).

The story of David's ascension to the throne was not an easy one. After his anointing by Samuel, the Lord used David to deliver the Israelites from a Philistine named Goliath, who had been holding the armies of the Lord in fear. The victory brought David great popularity among the people, but it came at a price, as Saul began to grow jealous and fear that David had plans to take the throne. Saul then attempted to kill David, forcing the younger man to flee for his life. David remained on the run for years. At one point, he learned that Saul had discovered that he and his men were hiding in the Desert of Ein Gedi and had sent an army to find him.

The way in which David learned this is quite humorous. The Bible states that Saul found a cave in the wilderness and went in to "relieve himself" (verse 3). But unknown to him, David and his army were hiding further back in the cave. David could have easily killed Saul, but he refused to take the life of the Lord's anointed, so instead he cut off a corner of Saul's robe. When Saul exited the cave, David followed him out and showed him the strip of cloth that he had taken. Saul wept aloud and declared, "You have treated me well, but I have treated you badly" (verse 17). He returned home and gave up the hunt for David . . . at least for a while.

Today, you can visit "David's Waterfall," located a mile from the entrance to the Ein Gedi Nature Reserve in Israel, where it is believed that David and his men camped out while on the run from Saul. From the foot of that waterfall, you can follow another path that leads to the Dudim Cave—which tradition holds is the same cave in which David spared Saul's life.[39]

C. In the Hebrew language, the word for *path* (*'egal*) literally means a circle.[40] The paths of righteousness that David refers to in Psalm 23:3 are thus circular in nature.

    1. In Israel (and other places), the sheep travel circular paths to go up hills. They don't go straight up because the climb is too hard. This is also true of the paths of righteousness.

    2. The Lord brings us on circular paths to lead us to green pastures. We may think, *Haven't I been this way before? Haven't I done this before?* But there is a reason that God leads us the way that he has chosen—just as he led David on "circular" paths in his story.

    3. We sometimes go around in circles in life, but if we didn't come around again, we wouldn't pick up people. We experience this life in the Lord together, going around and sharing.

IV. What can we learn through David's story about waiting on God and remaining faithful to him?

    A. David, like many other people in the Bible, had to wait for God's promise to be fulfilled.

        1. Biblical scholars believe that David actually waited between *fifteen* to *seventeen* years from the time he was anointed by Samuel to the time that he became king of Israel.

        2. There is a place you can visit called David's Waterfall. This is the "green pasture" where God led David as he traveled along the circular paths of righteousness. He was there alone, and sometimes with his men and family, protected from Saul in the wilderness.

3. David had to persevere and trust that God was in control in spite of the enemy's efforts to discourage him, dissuade him, and cause him to quit. God was developing resiliency and tenacity in David so he could be the warrior king the people of Israel needed.

B. David was not always perfect in walking the paths of righteousness. The Bible reveals that after he became king, he engaged in sins that brought tragedy to his family.

1. The story opens as follows: "In the spring, at the time when kings go off to war, David sent Joab out with the king's men and the whole Israelite army. They destroyed the Ammonites and besieged Rabbah. But David remained in Jerusalem" (2 Samuel 11:1).

2. David should have been at war. But instead he went out on his terrace, saw a woman (named Bathsheba) bathing, and committed adultery with her (see 2 Samuel 11:2–4).

3. David ultimately arranged for Bathsheba's husband to be killed in battle to cover his sin (see 2 Samuel 11:5–24). This sin led to tragedy in David's household (see 2 Samuel 13–15).

C. There is so much more in David's story that we could explore. But in the end, we can say that even though David was just a lowly shepherd, the Lord *saw* his heart and raised him up to be king. Even though he wasn't perfect, he walked the path of righteousness.

Discuss | 35 minutes

Take some time to discuss what you just watched by answering the following questions. There are some suggested questions below to help you begin your discussion, but feel free to pick any of the additional questions as time allows.

Suggested Questions

1. One of the more amusing aspects of David's anointing is that the Lord didn't specifically tell Samuel which of Jesse's sons would be king. Samuel saw Eliab, the oldest, and thought the Lord would surely anoint him. But God said, "People look at the outward appearance, but the LORD looks at the heart" (1 Samuel 16:7). What does it mean that God looks at "the heart" when it comes to the people he uses for his plans?

2. David was actually out tending his father's flocks when Samuel made his visit to the family. As a shepherd, he protected the sheep against predators like lions and bears. What do you think David learned about worship and depending on God in this role? How did this enable him to endure the trials he would face after his anointing?

3. Read John 10:9–10. In ancient Israel there was no door for the sheep in a pen, so a shepherd like David would have lain across the opening to keep the sheep in and the enemies out. In this way, the shepherd literally laid down his life for the sheep. How did Jesus use this analogy to describe the reason that he came into this world?

4. David waited between fifteen to seventeen years from the time of his anointing to the time he actually became king. During this time, he was often on the run for his

life, hiding in the wilderness and even in enemy territory. Why do you think God made David wait this long? How has he used seasons of waiting like this in your life?

Additional Questions

5. Read Acts 13:16–22. Centuries after David, people were still talking about him. In this instance, Paul was speaking to a group of Jews in the synagogue in Pisidian Antioch, reminding them of their history and revealing how Jesus was the promised Messiah. What did Paul say about David? What particular trait in David stood out to God?

6. Read Romans 1:28–32. In this passage, Paul discusses how God will give over those who choose to be continually unrepentant "to a depraved mind." In the case of King Saul, his continual disobedience led to God's covering of protection being lifted from him. What happened as a result—and how did it directly impact David's situation?

7. The Hebrew root word for *paths* in Psalm 23:3 is the same word used to describe someone walking in a circular way.[41] How does this describe the route that God often requires us to take when it comes to walking along the paths of righteousness?

8. Not even David was perfect in walking along God's paths of righteousness. What particular set of sins did he commit that brought tragedy to his family? How does it help you to know that in spite of David's incredible failures, the Lord still chose to use him?

Respond | 10 minutes

Review the outline for the video teaching and any notes you took. In the space below, write down your most significant takeaway from this session.

Pray | 10 minutes

End your time by praying together, asking the Lord to continue to lead you along his paths of righteousness. Ask if anyone has any prayer requests to share. Write those requests down in the space below so you and your group members can pray about them in the week ahead.

Name	Request

Personal Study

As you discussed this week, David was not the most likely candidate to be chosen as king. He was the youngest of Jesse's eight sons, and his father didn't even think it worthwhile to call him in from the fields where he was out tending the sheep. Yet God looked past all outward appearances and saw in David a humble servant who followed after him. David truly was "a man after [God's] own heart" and led God's people as a good shepherd. As you explore these themes this week, write down your responses to the questions in the spaces provided, as you will be given a few minutes to share your insights at the start of the next session. If you are reading *The God of the Way* alongside this study, first review chapter 11 in the book.

Day 1

God Looks at the Heart

*D*on't ever judge a book by its cover. How many times have you heard that saying? How many times have you failed to heed its warning? We judge "books" by their "covers" all the time. We make decisions about people based on their appearance and their personality. We judge other people by the possessions they own or the talents that they have. We judge ourselves based on our own idea of "covers"—our bodies, success, and wealth. But God doesn't care about any of these things.

When Samuel visited the home of a man named Jesse to anoint one of his sons as the next king of Israel, the prophet did not assume, based on appearance or status, that it would be David. He actually thought it would be Eliab, the oldest son, who on the exterior must have been an impressive figure like Saul. David was actually the smallest in stature, the youngest of eight sons, and a shepherd—which was a very humble job. God knew what Samuel's assumption would be and said to him, "Do not consider [Eliab's] appearance or his height, for I have rejected him" (1 Samuel 16:7).

God instead chose David—and he appears to have chosen him for one central reason: *David had a good heart.* In contrast to Saul, whom God had rejected as the leader of his people by this time, David was humble. He was young and teachable. As the youngest of Jesse's eight sons, he was likely not accustomed to leading or being in charge. While this may be in contrast with what we think is required of a leader today—experience, confidence, a big personality—God looked inside David, and he liked what he saw.

How many times have you been fooled by the book's "cover"? How many times have you been deceived by appearances? How many times have you rushed to judgment because of something you saw on the surface? The man who was so successful but not very kind. The woman who was so charismatic but lacked empathy. The couple who seemed so powerful and confident but only looked out for themselves. We may be duped by the cover from time to time, but God is never duped. He sees straight through it all.

Read | 1 Samuel 16:6–13

Reflect

1. Eliab was the eldest of Jesse's eight sons. Why do you think Samuel believed that Eliab must be God's anointed one? How did God respond to Samuel's assumption?

2. When God had rejected all seven of Jesse's sons, the bewildered Samuel asked if he had any others. Jesse answered, "There is still the youngest . . . he is tending the sheep" (1 Samuel 16:11). What happened to David after Samuel anointed him with oil? What do you think his brothers were thinking as they watched David being anointed?

3. Think about a time you judged someone on their outward appearance—whether that was on his or her looks, possessions, or status. What did you initially think based on that person's outward appearance? Were you right or wrong about that individual?

4. When have you been wrongfully judged based on your outward appearance? If God were to look at your heart today, what would he find in you?

Pray | As your prayer today, read the following lines from Psalm 139:23–24, written by King David: "Search me, God, and know my heart; test me and know my anxious thoughts. See if there is any offensive way in me, and lead me in the way everlasting."

-Day 2-

Waiting to Be Crowned

David did not become king overnight. Most scholars believe he had to wait fifteen to seventeen years to be crowned. In the meantime, he spent a lot of time running from Saul, who was jealous of him. He hid in caves and lived a life counter to the one a king leads.

David recorded his thoughts and feelings during this time in many of the psalms. Often, these took the form of a lament. For instance, as he wrote in Psalm 22:1–2, "My God, my God, why have you forsaken me? Why are you so far from saving me, so far from my cries of anguish? My God, I cry out by day, but you do not answer, by night, but I find no rest."

You have probably asked similar questions. Maybe God made a promise to you long ago that has yet to be fulfilled. Maybe you are waiting to be healed, or waiting on a promotion, or waiting for a child to come back to God. But nothing seems to be happening, and you wonder how much longer the Lord will make you wait. Waiting requires patience, trust, and hope, and when you've been waiting a long time, all of those can run on short supply.

Notice that something David *didn't* do during his tumultuous years of waiting was suppress or deny the difficulty and darkness that he felt. His psalms, while often full of praise and joy, are also filled with anguish, sadness, and despair. David understood that he could feel both at once. He could feel joy in the almighty God, but at the same time, he could feel overwhelmed by grief for his situation. Often, we think we can feel only one or the other. We can't praise God and lament at the same time. But, as evidenced by the psalm of David that you will study today, this simply isn't true. Praise and lament can coexist in our spirits.

Read | Psalm 13:1–6

Reflect

1. The phrase "how long" is used more times in this psalm than in any other single text in Scripture.[42] What are some of the things that David asks the Lord "how long" he

will have to wait to see resolved in his life? What do all these "how long" questions say about how David was feeling when he wrote this psalm?

2. Notice that David's sentiments in the psalm take a sharp turn in tone in verses 5-6. Why do you think David's attitude shifted so suddenly?

3. What are you waiting on today that has often made you ask the Lord, *"How long?"* What has this waiting process been like for you and your loved ones?

4. What thoughts or feelings have you suppressed around this circumstance—whether that is lament or praise? How could you express those thoughts and feelings now?

Pray | Be honest with God during your prayer time. Let yourself feel a range of emotions rather than suppressing negative or positive ones. End your prayer in praise, knowing that you can praise the Lord in the midst of lament. You don't have to wait until the season of grief is over.

-Day 3-

The Mighty Will Fall

In an age of "cancel culture," we are not naive about leaders' failures. The higher one rises in power and fame, the greater the fall. David was not immune to this type of failure. While God chose him for his humble heart, David's pride would fail him as a leader.

Perhaps the most famous example of David's failure is found in the story of Bathsheba (see 2 Samuel 11). It is important to note the power dynamic between David and Bathsheba in this account. David was a man and the king. Bathsheba was a woman who had no rights outside of her husband and held no political status. Because of this, Bathsheba would not have had a choice in turning down David's command. Consent was the only option. David compounded the tragedy by having her husband, Uriah, killed in battle.

While the Bible often depicts David as a hero, in this particular story we see the hero's fatal flaw on full display. He is not immune. He is not perfect. He is not God. David would definitely have been canceled in today's culture. This part of David's story needs no excuses. We don't have to explain away David's behavior. And this part of David's story does not need to be covered up or forgotten about. In fact, it would not have been included in the pages of the Bible if it didn't serve a purpose—if it didn't contain a moral lesson for us.

So, instead of trying to clean up David's story, we can sit with the tension. David failed his people and his God, and it does not serve us to look away or sweep those truths under the rug. David certainly did not. As you will see in the psalm you will study today, David once again turned to writing out his laments and asking God for forgiveness.

Read | Psalm 51:1–9

Reflect

1. David wrote this psalm after the prophet Nathan reprimanded him for murdering Uriah and taking Bathsheba as his wife. Nathan also told David that he would be

punished for his sins—his son with Bathsheba would not survive (see 2 Samuel 12:13–14). How does David describe himself in this passage? How does he describe God?

2. According to this psalm, how did David feel about his crimes against Bathsheba and Uriah? How did David feel about the possibility of receiving mercy from God?

3. When has someone you respected fallen from grace? How did it make you feel about that person and impact your relationship? Explain your response.

4. The Lord forgave David in spite of his many failures. Did you feel like the person in your situation deserved this kind of forgiveness? Why or why not?

Pray | During your prayer time today, ask God for what you need—whether that is forgiveness for someone else or forgiveness for yourself. Trust that he is the God described in this psalm: a God of mercy, of unfailing love, and of great compassion.

- Day 4 -

The Good Shepherd

It's never easy when a leader we love fails us. It's tempting to abandon that leader altogether—and sometimes walking away is necessary, depending on the nature of the offense. But when this person is a leader of a church or a ministry, things can get more complicated. We can sometimes confuse walking away from a leader who failed us with walking away from our faith.

As we have seen, David failed while he was king—and he did so more than once. But his failure is meant to point us to Someone greater. It is telling that Jesus was a direct descendent in the line of David. Just as David was a shepherd—first literally and then as the caretaker of God's people—so Jesus described himself as a shepherd. Just as David was a king. so Jesus is the King of kings. Jesus is the true and better David—a leader who will never fail us. He is "the good shepherd" (John 10:11) who always protects us and guides us.

History is littered with the failures of leaders of the faith. There are leaders who have abused the gospel and used it for their own gain. There are those who have used the Bible as a weapon and to keep people in bondage instead of setting them free. But this is why we don't worship pastors, ministry leaders, or any other leader of the faith. We worship only Jesus, the one true King and Shepherd.

When all other leaders fall, we can look to Jesus and see that he is still seated on the throne of God. His love, grace, and compassion will *never* fail us.

Read | John 10:7–11

Reflect

1. Jesus spoke these words to a group of Pharisees (Jewish religious leaders) after he had healed a man born blind (see John 9). The Pharisees couldn't believe that Jesus had healed on the *Sabbath*, so they threw the once-blind man out of the synagogue—the

equivalent of ostracizing him from society. Considering this context, what do you think Jesus meant in John 10:9? What message was he trying to send to the Pharisees?

2. Jesus said, "The thief comes only to steal and kill and destroy; I have come that they may have life, and have it to the full" (verse 10). What does this imply that a good shepherd/leader does? How does this differ from the way they were treating the man?

3. Jesus is the only perfect leader of our faith. How does his leadership differ from the "Pharisees" that you've encountered in your faith community?

4. How have you been hurt by a "Pharisee" or a pharisaical attitude in the church? What do you think Jesus would have to say about the pain you have experienced?

Pray | Church hurt is real. If you've been around the community of faith long enough, you will eventually experience it. Bring this pain before Jesus today, whether it is recent or from your past. Lay your grief and/or anger at his feet. Allow the Good Shepherd to heal you.

– Day 5 –

Intimacy with God

Inevitably, in any long-term relationship, there will be conflict. You will disagree with the other person. The two of you will fight. You will get angry at each other. Then, after time has passed and you've been able to talk things through, you will reconcile. After this reconciliation, it's likely you will feel even closer to this person than you did before.

While you might avoid conflict in relationships, it can bring you to a deeper level of intimacy with the other person. Conflict means that you are being honest about your needs. It means you are willing to find out how the other person feels even if it hurts you. When you avoid hard conversations, you miss out on deeper connections with those you love.

David had an intimate relationship with God. We know this from his story told in the Bible and through his psalms. But his intimacy with the Lord only came through honesty. David cried out to God when he felt abandoned. David expressed his sorrow when God reprimanded him for his failings. David begged the Lord for mercy, forgiveness, and deliverance from his enemies.

David's relationship with God was honest—and therefore it was intimate.

What is your relationship like with God? Does *intimate* describe it? Maybe *distant* or *formal* is a better descriptor. It's easy to grow distant from God and neglect the spiritual practices that keep you connected to him.

Fortunately, God never grows distant from *you*. He is always there, waiting for you to call on him. When you draw near to him, he draws near to you.

Read | Psalm 119:97–104 and James 4:8–10

Reflect

1. While the author of Psalm 119 is unknown, many scholars believe it was written by David. (It also could have been written by Ezra or Daniel.) How does the psalmist feel

about God's Word? What does this tell you about the power of God's Word when it comes to being in relationship with the Lord?

2. According to James, what will happen when you come near to God and humble yourself before him? Practically speaking, what does it look like to come near to God in humility?

3. How would you describe your relationship with God today?

4. What do you admire the most about God and David's relationship? How do you think you could achieve this in your relationship with God?

Pray | Spend time in God's Word today as you pray. You could read through the passages above or another passage that helps you feel intimate with God. Draw near to him through his Word, knowing that he will draw near to you.

For Next Week

Before you meet again with your group this week, read chapter 12 of *The God of the Way*. Also go back and complete any of the study and reflection questions from this personal study that you weren't able to finish.

Schedule

WEEK 6

BEFORE GROUP MEETING	Read chapter 12 in *The God of the Way* Read the Welcome section (page 133)
GROUP MEETING	Discuss the Connect questions Watch the video teaching for session 6 Discuss the questions that follow as a group Do the closing exercise and pray (pages 133–144)
PERSONAL STUDY – DAY 1	Complete the daily study (pages 146–147)
PERSONAL STUDY – DAY 2	Complete the daily study (pages 148–149)
PERSONAL STUDY – DAY 3	Complete the daily study (pages 150–151)
PERSONAL STUDY – DAY 4	Complete the daily study (pages 152–153)
PERSONAL WRAP-UP	Complete the daily study (pages 154–155) Connect with your group about the next study that you want to go through together

Mary of Magdala

GOD SEES US IN OUR GRIEF

At this, [Mary] turned around and saw Jesus standing there,
but she did not realize that it was Jesus. He asked her, "Woman,
why are you crying? Who is it you are looking for?" Thinking
he was the gardener, she said, "Sir, if you have carried him away,
tell me where you have put him, and I will get him." Jesus said
to her, "Mary." She turned toward him and cried out in Aramaic,
"Rabboni!" (which means "Teacher").

JOHN 20:14–16

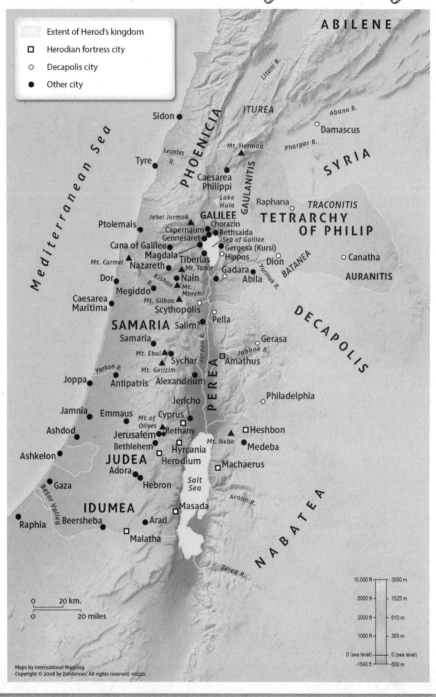

Israel in Mary's Day

Legend:
- Extent of Herod's kingdom
- □ Herodian fortress city
- ○ Decapolis city
- ● Other city

ABILENE

Mediterranean Sea

PHOENICIA
ITUREA
SYRIA

Sidon
Tyre
Leontes R.
Litani R.
Abana R.
Damascus
Mt. Hermon
Pharpar R.
Caesarea Philippi
GAULANITIS
Lake Hula
Raphana
TRACONITIS
TETRARCHY OF PHILIP
Ptolemais
Jebel Jarmak
GALILEE
Chorazin
Capernaum
Bethsaida
Gennesaret
Cana of Galilee
Sea of Galilee
Gergesa (Kursi)
Magdala
Hippos
Canatha
Mt. Carmel
Tiberias
Dion
BATANEA
Nazareth
Mt. Tabor
Gadara
AURANITIS
Dor
Nain
Mt. Moreh
Abila
Yarmuk R.
Kishon R.
Megiddo
Mt. Gilboa
Caesarea Maritima
Scythopolis
DECAPOLIS
Salim?
Pella
SAMARIA
Samaria
Gerasa
Mt. Ebal
Sychar
Jabbok R.
Amathus
Mt. Gerizim
Yarkon R.
Joppa
Antipatris
Alexandrium
PEREA
Jericho
Philadelphia
Jamnia
Emmaus
Cyprus
Mt. of Olives
Ashdod
Jerusalem
Bethany
Bethlehem
Hyrcania
Mt. Nebo
Heshbon
Ashkelon
JUDEA
Herodium
Medeba
Adora
Machaerus
Gaza
Hebron
Salt Sea
Besor Valley
IDUMEA
Arnon R.
Raphia
Beersheba
Masada
Arad
NABATEA
Malatha
Zered R.

20 km.
20 miles

10,000 ft — 3050 m
5000 ft — 1525 m
2000 ft — 610 m
1000 ft — 305 m
0 (sea level) — 0 (sea level)
-1640 ft — -500 m

Welcome | Read On Your Own

In the last session, you looked at the story of David. You saw that even though he was the youngest of Jesse's eight sons—and even though he was not even present when the prophet Samuel came to his family's home—the Lord saw him as he was out tending his father's flocks. God selected him to be the next king of Israel because of his heart.

In this world, we can feel unseen and overlooked the way David must have felt. It can seem as if we are just one face in the sea of many. We are suffering, but nobody notices. We are sick, but nobody seems to want to help. We are lonely, but everyone is too busy with their own lives to stop in and see us. Perhaps this is how Mary of Magdala, the woman we will study in this final session, felt about herself before she met Jesus. She was simply another woman in the crowd, afflicted and alone. The Bible relates that she was possessed by seven demons. But as far as we know, no one came to her aid until she met Jesus.

Mary's encounter with the Messiah forever transformed her life. She was healed of the demons and became his faithful follower. She supported his ministry financially and never left his side—not during his ministry, not while he hung on the cross, and not even after he was buried. In fact, all the Gospels report that it was Mary, along with other women, who was the first to see the empty tomb and realize that Jesus had risen from the dead. But Mary is unique in that when Jesus encountered her in the garden by his tomb, he called her by name.

Jesus also calls you by name so that you, like Mary, may have the hope of resurrection in your life. Her story reveals that we are never too sick, or too afflicted, or too much of an outcast for God to see us. He will never leave us or forsake us (see Hebrews 13:5–6).

Connect | 15 minutes

Welcome to session 6 of *The God Who Sees*. To get things started for this week's final group time, discuss one of the following questions:

- What is a key insight or takeaway from last week's personal study that you would like to share with the group?

— *or* —

- When is a time that you felt like an outsider because of a struggle or affliction in your life? How did God reveal himself to you during that time?

Watch | 20 minutes

Now watch the video for this session. As you watch, use the following outline to record any thoughts or concepts that stand out to you.

I. What are some of the unique aspects of Mary of Magdala as a follower of Jesus?

    A. Mary of Magdala played a huge role in the epic story of God's love. But there is a lot of misunderstanding today about Mary's situation before she encountered the Messiah.

        1. Several hundred years after Jesus, people in the church begin writing about Mary of Magdala and saying that she was a prostitute before she met Jesus.

        2. What happened is that these individuals began merging the stories of the woman with the alabaster jar who anointed Jesus in Luke 7:37 with Mary of Magdala.

        3. The connection stuck, and she was labeled a "sinful woman." But there is no proof from the account of her life given in the Gospels that she was ever a prostitute.

    B. Mary was one of the women who accompanied and aided Jesus in his ministry (see Luke 8:1–2). Each of the Gospels also attests that she witnessed Jesus' crucifixion and burial.

        1. The Gospel of John further notes that Mary stood by the cross near the virgin Mary—near the mother of Jesus—when Jesus spoke to John (see John 19:25–26).

        2. Mary ended up as one of the most profound people in all of the New Testament. She, just like Lazarus and his sisters, had a close and intimate relationship with Jesus.

The Number Seven in Scripture

The Hebrew word for seven (*sheba* or *shibah*) carries a meaning that goes beyond a mere numerical value. This is because one of the Hebrew root words used in the term is *saba*, which carries with it the meaning of *fullness, wholeness, abundance*, and *completeness*.[43] The following are a few examples from Scripture of how the number seven is used in this manner.

Creation. In the story of creation, God forms the heavens and the earth in six days and then rests on the seventh day. "By the seventh day God had finished the work he had been doing; so on the seventh day he rested from all his work" (Genesis 2:2). The Lord rested on the *seventh* day because his work was *finished* and *complete*.

Noah. When God sent Noah into the ark, he said, "Take with you seven pairs of every kind of clean animal, a male and its mate . . . and also seven pairs of every kind of bird, male and female" (Genesis 7:2–3). Noah was to offer a sacrifice after the flood, so the extra animals were needed to ensure the species could repopulate the earth. These seven animals would be a symbol of God's *abundance* to Noah and indicate that his judgment was *complete*.

Jericho. During the conquest of Canaan, God gave these instructions to Joshua on how to capture the first city of Jericho: "March around the city once with all the armed men. Do this for six days. Have seven priests carry trumpets of rams' horns in front of the ark. On the seventh day, march around the city seven times, with the priests blowing the trumpets. When you hear them sound a long blast on the trumpets, have the whole army give a loud shout; then the wall of the city will collapse and the army will go up, everyone straight in" (Joshua 6:3–5). The repetition of the number *seven* indicated that God was giving the land *completely* to them.

Forgiveness. When Peter asked Jesus if he should forgive a brother or sister who had sinned against him "up to seven times," the Lord answered, "I tell you, not seven times, but seventy-seven times" (Matthew 18:21–22). Peter thought he was being generous with his offer of seven times, but Jesus' multiplication of the number seven implies that we are to be *abundant* in our grace to others and forgive them *wholly, fully*, and *completely*.[44]

3. Mary actually supported Jesus' ministry financially. She had means of some kind, possibly because she came from a prominent family, though the Bible doesn't say.

C. Mary was one of the few female disciples mentioned in the Gospels.

1. Mary had strong faith and a desperate longing to be close to Jesus. She wanted to be near Jesus wherever he traveled—to sit and learn at his feet.

2. While the Bible doesn't give us many details about Mary's life before she met Jesus, we do know that she was delivered from seven demons (see Luke 8:2).

3. We can just imagine that Jesus' words were like honey and balm to Mary after living in the darkness for so long (see Proverbs 16:24).

II. What is the significance of Mary being delivered from *seven* demons?

A. We do not know how long Mary struggled with being possessed by seven demons.

1. We also do not know how old Mary was when she met Jesus. Given that men were not allowed to become rabbis until age thirty, she was likely his contemporary.

2. Regardless of when she came to Jesus, it would have been long enough for seven demons to find a comfortable place to live. But why *seven*?

B. The number seven in Hebrew represents fullness or completion. It completes a cycle.

    1. One scholar surmises that this may mean that Mary of Magdala suffered the most severe emotional and psychological trauma because of the "seven" demons.

    2. In many cases, seven is a good thing in Scripture . . . even a great thing. But in Mary's case, it meant that the demons had full possession and control over her.

C. The Bible delineates between those who are mentally ill and those who are demonized.

    1. Believers in some parts of the world say, "There's a demon under every rock." Believers in other parts say, "There is nothing demonic anywhere." Both are unbiblical.

    2. Just as the presence of the Holy Spirit is everywhere, so demonic presence is everywhere. The enemy is described as "the ruler of the kingdom of the air" (Ephesians 2:2).

    3. There are eighty references in the Bible to demons. But there are eleven specific references that denote clear distinctions between physical illness and illnesses that are caused by demonization.

D. It is thus incorrect to say that all mental illness is caused by demonization. We have to know God—and have intimacy with him—to be able to discern the difference.

    1. We have chemical imbalances in the brain. We have fallen bodies. We have all kinds of ways that we become sick. We can become sick in body and sick in mind.

    2. So it is not all caused by demonization, but demons do possess, oppress, and harass.

3. An important verse we need to know: "We know that anyone born of God does not continue to sin; the One who was born of God keeps them safe, and the evil one cannot harm them" (1 John 5:18). So a person who is a follower of Jesus cannot be possessed.

III. What does the Bible reveal about Mary's presence at Jesus' crucifixion and resurrection?

A. The Gospels state that Mary, the mother of Jesus; Mary of Magdala; other women; and the disciple John were all present at Jesus' crucifixion.

1. It is difficult to imagine watching a crucifixion. But these individuals stayed there and watched the one they loved being tortured on the cross until he gave up his last breath.

2. John was the only male disciple of Jesus who was present. Jesus said to him, "Woman, here is your son" (John 19:26). Mary had other children by that time, but Jesus wanted his mother to be cared for by one who knew him and recognized him as the Messiah.

3. All of Jesus' followers were broken. They had been loving this man they believed to be the Messiah. But now all of their hopes and dreams seemed to be at an end.

B. Women were the only individuals to visit Jesus' tomb on Sunday morning. At dawn, Mary and the other women set out to anoint Jesus' body (see John 20:1).

1. Mary knew there would be Roman soldiers. She knew that Jesus was an enemy of the state and an enemy of the Jewish religious leaders. She had tremendous courage.

Accounts of the Resurrection

The accounts of the resurrection reveal that there was a great deal of confusion and excitement when the disciples learned Jesus' tomb was empty. The Gospel writers did not try to capture every detail of the resurrection or even present a chronological listing of what happened, so the accounts can seem out of harmony. But here is what could be the sequence of events.

First, Jesus is buried in the tomb of Joseph of Arimathea (see Matthew 27:57–61; Mark 15:42–47; Luke 23:50–56; John 19:38–42). The tomb is sealed and a guard set (see Matthew 27:62–66). At least three women—Mary of Magdala, Mary the mother of James, and Salome—prepare to go to the tomb (see Matthew 28:1; Mark 16:1). Meanwhile, an angel appears and rolls away the stone. His presence is accompanied by a great earthquake that causes the guards to tremble and become like dead men (see Matthew 28:2–4).

The women arrive at the tomb and find it empty. Mary of Magdala leaves the other women and runs to tell the disciples (see John 20:1–2). The women who remain encounter two angels, who tell them that Jesus is risen (see Matthew 28:5-7; Mark 16:2–8; Luke 24:1–8). These women leave to tell the disciples (see Matthew 28:8). On the way, they see Jesus (see Matthew 28:9–10). The women carry all this news back to the disciples (see Luke 24:9–11).

Meanwhile, Mary of Magdala tells Peter and John that the tomb is empty (see John 20:1–2). They run to the tomb to see for themselves (see Luke 24:12; John 20:3–10). Mary follows after, arrives at the tomb, sees the angels, and then encounters Jesus (see John 20:11–18). Later that day, Jesus appears to Peter (see Luke 24:34) and then to the disciples on the road to Emmaus (see Luke 24:13–32). Sometime later, he appears to all the disciples except Thomas (see Luke 24:36–43; John 20:19–25), and then to all eleven (see John 20:26–31).

Finally, Jesus appears to seven disciples at the Sea of Galilee (see John 21:1–25), then to 500 disciples in Galilee (see 1 Corinthians 15:6), and then to his half-brother James (see 1 Corinthians 15:7). Jesus then ascends into heaven (see Luke 24:50–53; Acts 1:6–12).

2. Mary would have begun her journey that Sunday morning, the minute the Jewish Sabbath law allowed her to carry things. She found the tomb empty and ran to get Peter and John. When they left, she saw someone in the hazy light whom she believed to be the gardener (see John 20:2–15).

3. Mary said, "Sir, if you have carried him away, tell me where you have put him, and I will get him" (John 20:15). She couldn't have lifted him up, but she wanted to be with him.

C. We don't know if Mary believed in the resurrection before this moment. But we do know that she believed in the resurrection after Jesus spoke her name.

1. The first word that Jesus said to her was simply, "Mary." When Mary heard her name, she immediately recognized Jesus and cried out, "Rabboni!" (John 20:16). Not because she could see him any better but because she knew her Shepherd's voice.

2. This is a precious example of our Savior's redemptive love. Jesus didn't say, "Oh, woman, you silly thing, it's me." He said—so lovingly, as he had many times before—"Mary."

3. Right now, Jesus is saying that to us. He is beseeching us to hear his voice. Even in the darkness of our lives—even in the shadows—he wants us to know that *he sees us*.

IV. What are some takeaways from Mary's story as it relates to God seeing our loved ones?

A. When we read of Mary's dedication to Jesus—how she followed him, supported him, and stayed with him at the cross—we recognize that Jesus had family members who did not believe in him.

    1. The same is true in our lives. Not all of us have family members who believe. Even more, not all of us have family members who want *us* to believe in Jesus.

    2. The testimony of our lives as followers of the Way—as followers of Jesus just like Mary—is to be love to these people in our lives. We let them see what love looks like.

B. So often in life, we meet people whom Jesus is calling by name. We know that he is calling them, but their ears are not open to hear his voice.

    1. These people in our lives may become upset with us. They call us "Jesus freaks" (or whatever) because we, like Mary, are devoted to Jesus.

    2. One of our biggest challenges is to not judge them in their weakness but to follow the example of Jesus, who loved everyone exactly the same and met them in their need.

C. Our part in sharing the good news of Jesus is often to simply plant a seed. We just love on one of God's other kids. When we do this, we reveal that there is a God who sees them.

Discuss | 35 minutes

Take some time to discuss what you just watched by answering the following questions. There are some suggested questions below to help you begin your discussion, but feel free to pick any of the additional questions as time allows.

Suggested Questions

1. Read Luke 8:1–3. Mary of Magdala and these other women traveled with Jesus and supported him financially. The Greek word that Luke uses in this passage to describe their activities is *diakoneo*, from which we get our modern English word *deacon*.[45] What does this say about the depth of their involvement in Jesus' ministry?

2. The number seven in Hebrew represents fullness or completion. We see the importance of the number seven in the Creation story, where God created for six days and then rested on the seventh day, because his work was complete (see Genesis 2:2). What is the significance of the number seven in Mary's story? What does the fact that she was possessed by seven demons say about the depth of her affliction?

3. In the Gospel of Mark, we read that when Jesus was arrested in the garden of Gethsemane, the disciples "deserted him and fled" (Mark 14:50). However, when Jesus was on the cross, the Gospel of John reveals that "near the cross of Jesus stood his mother, his mother's sister, Mary the wife of Clopas, and Mary Magdalene" (John 19:25). What were Mary and the other women risking by being present at the cross?

4. Each of the Gospels reveals that Mary of Magdala was devoted to Jesus throughout his ministry. What lessons have you learned from her story about God's desire to

use those who are on the "fringes"—those outcast from culture and society—in his plans for the world?

Additional Questions

5. Read Luke 7:36–38. One of the misunderstandings about Mary that has come down through the history of the church is that she was the woman referenced in this passage who "lived a sinful life." Why do you think she was associated with this woman? How has this served to diminish how we think of her as a disciple of Jesus?

6. In Ephesians 6:12, Paul writes that "our struggle is not against flesh and blood, but against the rulers, against the authorities, against the powers of this dark world and against the spiritual forces of evil in the heavenly realms." What does this say about the forces of darkness that are at work in our world today? While it is unbiblical to say that *everything* bad that happens is a result of demonic forces, why is it equally unbiblical to say that *nothing* bad that happens is a result of Satan's forces at work?

7. When you read the story of Mary at the empty tomb, it is evident she was distraught and feared the authorities had taken his body away. It does *not* appear that she had considered the possibility of his resurrection. Why do you think Jesus asked why she was crying and who it was she was looking for before he revealed himself to her?

8. Read Matthew 12:46–50. Unlike Mary of Magdala and Jesus' disciples, it does not appear that all of his family members believed that he was the Messiah (at least, not until after his resurrection). What does Jesus say in this passage about whom he considers to be his family? What encouragement does this give you today?

Respond | 10 minutes

Review the outline for the video teaching and any notes you took. In the space below, write down your most significant takeaway from this session.

Pray | 10 minutes

End your time by praying together, thanking Jesus for inviting you to be a member of his own family. Ask if anyone has any prayer requests to share. Write those requests down in the space below so you and your group members can pray about them in the week ahead.

Name	Request

Personal Study

As you have seen throughout this study, we serve a *God who sees* us in each and every situation in our lives. Mary of Magdala was tormented by seven demons and lived in a world of darkness. She must have wondered if God saw her in her plight . . . and if he cared. But when she met Jesus, she was delivered from demonic possession, and her life was never the same. She did what all people do when they encounter the Messiah—she became his faithful follower. As you explore these themes in the story of Mary of Magdala this week, be sure to write down your responses to the questions in the spaces provided. If you are reading *The God of the Way* alongside this study, first review chapter 12 in the book.

-Day 1-

Complete Freedom

Mary of Magdala appears quite subtly on the pages of the Bible. The first we hear about her is a casual reference to the fact that at some point, in a story not told in Scripture, she was possessed with seven demons and then healed by Jesus (see Luke 8:2). What is not said leaves us with many questions. *When did Jesus heal her? How did he heal her? What was she like as a woman possessed by demons? Did all seven demons come out at once?*

Of course, these questions are not answered in the Bible, but we can infer from cultural context that Mary's being possessed left her ostracized from her community. The number seven is symbolic in Jewish tradition, indicating completeness.[46] Mary was likely completely possessed by these demonic forces, which would not have allowed her to live a normal life. The number seven is also symbolic of rest, meaning that Jesus cast all seven demons out of her and completely freed Mary of her affliction.[47] She was finally—after who knows how many years—able to rest in the type of freedom only Jesus can give.

Unfortunately, both demonic possession and affliction are still commonplace. And we have all been afflicted by something at some point in our lives. We have also all likely experienced *total* affliction—feeling consumed by sin, addiction, anxiety, depression, fear, mental illness, anger, or something else. We wonder if we will ever be free.

Mary Magdalene gives hope to the afflicted. A person could not have been more consumed by evil than she was, and yet her demons were no match for Jesus. Because of her story, you can trust that your afflictions are no match for Jesus either.

Read | Galatians 5:1 and 1 John 5:18–20

Reflect

1. Paul, the author of Galatians, was on a mission to educate and encourage the early church. He emphasized to the believers in Galatia that they had been saved by grace

and not by any works of the law. What do you think he meant when he said, "It is for freedom that Christ has set us free"? To what type of freedom is he referring?

2. According to 1 John 5:18, even though evil controls the world, why do we not have to be afraid? How does Mary of Magdala embody the truth of these passages?

3. Think about any afflictions that you are confronting today. How has this affliction affected you spiritually, emotionally, or physically?

4. What hope do these passages (as well as Mary's story) give you in the face of this affliction? Do you believe freedom is possible for you? Why or why not?

Pray | Lift your affliction up to the one true healer today. The one who freed Mary *completely* from her *complete* affliction can do the same for you. Ask the Lord for hope and for healing. Healing may not happen miraculously overnight—sometimes healing is long, slow work. But no matter what it looks like or how long it takes, Jesus is with you every step of the way.

- Day 2 -

Disciples of Jesus

Jesus wasn't known for hanging out with the rich and powerful. In fact, he often kept company with the opposite: fishermen, the sick, disabled, demoniacs, and women. In particular, to keep company with women at this time was scandalous. For women to learn from Jesus alongside men was even more scandalous. Coeducation was unheard of in first-century Israel.[48] This is why Mary of Magdala would have likely caused a stir with her connection to Jesus. When we are introduced to her, she is traveling with him, along with several other women who are helping support his ministry (see Luke 8:2–3).

When we think of Jesus' disciples, the names Peter, Andrew, James, John, and the other Twelve come to mind. But Mary of Magdala, and these other women, were his followers and his disciples too. Jesus didn't discriminate based on social class, physical ability, or gender. If someone was devoted to him, that person could learn from him.

Our world is not always so welcoming. As a woman, a person of color, or someone who is not able-bodied, maybe you have experienced closed doors in places you hoped would be open: a church, a school, a workplace. Even if you're not part of a marginalized group, you also know what it's like to not be given the same opportunities as someone else based on something about you that you have no control over and cannot change. It's part of the human experience. Fortunately, Jesus of Nazareth felt differently. He shifted the paradigms and did the unexpected. He accepted and taught women. He reached into the margins and pulled others in rather than keeping them out. In Jesus' family, anyone can be a disciple.

Read | Luke 10:25–37

Reflect

1. In this passage, Jesus answered a question by an expert in the law with a story about a good Samaritan. Jews had no dealings with Samaritans at this time (see John 4:9).

They were considered unclean. How do you think the man felt about Jesus' answer to his question, "Who is my neighbor?" How are we supposed to love our neighbor?

2. When you read this passage, what does it say about the importance of loving your neighbor? Why do you think God wants you to love others in this way?

3. Who is your "neighbor"—the person on the fringes of your community who has less opportunity than you because of their gender, social status, or race? How is this person treated by those around you? How do you feel about this neighbor?

4. When have *you* felt like the neighbor—receiving a closed door because of something about you, your body, your family, or background? How did this make you feel? How could this moment give you empathy for the neighbors you are called to love?

Pray | Think about Jesus' care for Mary of Magdala and the other women. Think about his care for *you*. You are his disciple. He is proud to bring you into his family. Pray about the places and spaces where you feel you don't belong. Ask Jesus who your neighbors are. Pray about how you could welcome one of those neighbors into your church or community.

Day 3

Called by Name

When is the last time that someone called you by name? Your real, full name? Hearing your own name can be powerful. It can make you feel seen and known. It can be intimate, depending on who is saying it. It can be a breath of fresh air when no one has called you by name in days or months. It can remind you of who you are. It can connect you with someone you haven't seen in a while or perhaps even thought that you would never see again.

What would it be like to hear Jesus speak your name? Mary of Magdala knows. Perhaps what Mary is best known for in Scripture is being the first to witness the risen Christ. From a woman possessed by seven demons to the first to witness the greatest miracle in history—Mary had indeed changed when she met Jesus. She arrived at his tomb not knowing he had risen. In her heart and mind, her Rabbi was gone—the one who saved her, the one who had mercy on her, the one who pulled her in from the margins and taught her. Her friend.

Mary didn't recognize Jesus at first. This is how far her mind was from expecting to see the risen Messiah that day. It wasn't until Jesus said one sweet word—"Mary"—that she knew exactly who he was. All of a sudden, it was as if she had been transported back to the first day they met, when Jesus saw her and healed her. Here he was again, doing the same.

Jesus sees you too. He knows your name. When you feel like no one cares, when you feel like no one knows you, when you feel alone—remember in the darkness of the garden and on the morning of your greatest grief, Jesus has called you by name.

Read | Isaiah 43:1 and John 20:11–16

Reflect

1. Isaiah prophesied that God would bring the Israelites back to himself after the Babylonian captivity. He would bring them back to Jerusalem. How did God reassure

his people in this passage? What do you think it the significance of him calling the Israelites by name?

2. How do you think Mary felt when she heard Jesus say her name? What did she call Jesus—and what does this tell you about their relationship?

3. How does it feel when the person you love the most and who knows you best calls you by name? (Maybe this is a spouse, parent, or friend—or maybe this is someone you lost and you wish you could hear him or her say your name again.)

4. God told the prophet Jeremiah, "Before I formed you in the womb I knew you, before you were born I set you apart; I appointed you as a prophet to the nations" (Jeremiah 1:5). Do you believe that God truly sees you and knows you in this way? If not, what is keeping you from believing this about him?

Pray | During your prayer time today, sit in silence for a few moments. Wait and listen for the voice of Jesus. Imagine that you are in the garden with him just as Mary was. Imagine he is saying your name. What would it mean to you if you heard this today?

Day 4

A Sense of Urgency

What do you do when you see a good movie, or read a good book, or hear an interesting story? If you are like most people, you go and tell others about it. But what do you do when you see a *really* good movie, or read a *really* good book, or hear one of the *most interesting* stories you've ever heard? Well, in that case, you likely go and tell others about it *immediately*.

This is what Mary did after she encountered the risen Jesus outside the tomb. She immediately went and told the others.

Mary was, in the famous words of Thomas Aquinas, "an apostle to the apostles."[49] She was the first witness to the resurrection and the first to tell the others about it. Of course, this doesn't mean that she was believed by the others. Some were skeptical. The news was just too good to be true. But Jesus would confirm his resurrection for them soon enough, appearing in their midst and proving to the most skeptical among them that he was alive (see John 20:19).

Mary had witnessed a miracle. She could not wait to tell others about it. Maybe you felt the same way the first time you heard about Jesus and his saving grace. Maybe you were shouting it from the rooftops and telling anyone who would listen. You were a new convert on fire for the Lord! But maybe you are now wondering what happened to that fire and that sense of urgency. You're more excited to tell people about the movie you just saw than about the risen Christ.

How easy it is to forget the miraculous nature of that resurrection moment.

Today, take a look again at the empty tomb. Consider the implication that Jesus' resurrection has on your life. Feel the urgency that Mary of Magdala felt to tell the others—the excitement, the wonder, the utter joy. Keep the miracle of Jesus' resurrection alive in your heart, and never stop telling the story. After all, you never know who needs to hear the message of the gospel today.

Read | John 20:17–18 and Luke 24:9–12

Reflect

1. All four Gospels share the story of Jesus' resurrection, but each account varies slightly and reveals different details. According to John's Gospel, what did Jesus tell Mary to do? What actions did she take in response to Jesus' words?

2. According to Luke's Gospel, who was skeptical of the women's story? Why do you think they didn't believe them? What did Peter think after he saw the empty tomb?

3. Think back on your own life and the first time you really heard someone else tell you about Jesus. If you were an adult, were you skeptical of the person or the story they told? If you were a child, what can you remember about first learning about Jesus?

4. Do you tend to find it easy or difficult to share about Jesus with others? How could Mary's story encourage you to keep spreading the message of the gospel?

Pray | Spend some time reflecting on the miracle of the resurrection. What does it mean to you today? What did it mean to you when you first became a Christian? Ask Jesus to restore your joy, awe, and wonder in this miracle and the miracle of his love and grace.

– Day 5 –

A Life of Devotion

*D*evotion is a strong word. It suggests commitment, consistency, and love. We only devote ourselves to something or someone to which we are willing to give all three. Maybe this is a spouse, or a child, or a person for whom we are a caregiver. Or maybe your devotion takes the form of commitment, consistency, and love toward a workout routine, job, or hobby.

The word *devotion* perfectly encompassed Mary of Magdala's relationship with Jesus. She was fully devoted to him, and with good reason. As we have seen, Jesus pulled her away from the evil one, healing her from seven demons. He gave her status among his disciples. He revealed himself to her after the resurrection and gave her these instructions: "Go. . . to my brothers and tell them, 'I am ascending to my Father and your Father, to my God and your God'" (John 20:17).

As one writer said, "Mary owed much, gave much, loved much, served much."[50]

Mary's devotion to Christ came naturally because he had given so much to her. But is the same true of our own devotion? Is the object of our devotion a thing or person that has given us something invaluable like love, acceptance, or a sense of self-worth?

The answer is likely sometimes *yes* and sometimes *no*. Sometimes we devote ourselves to something or someone in the *hope* that the person or thing will give us something in return. Sometimes, our devotion stems from what we have already received. This latter type of devotion is the lasting kind. It doesn't take effort. It is an overflow—a continuous act of gratitude.

Mary was devoted to Jesus in his life, in his death, and in his resurrection. Unlike so many of the things on which we focus our devotion, Mary knew that her life had been transformed and that Jesus was the one true thing in life worthy of her devotion. So she never left Jesus' side, even when many of the others did.

Her devotion to Jesus was steadfast until the very end.

Read | Matthew 27:45–56; Mark 16:1–4; and 2 Corinthians 5:13–15

Reflect

1. According to Matthew's account of Jesus' crucifixion, where was Mary when Jesus died? According to Mark's account, what did Mary do the Sunday after Jesus' death?

2. Paul wrote, "Christ's love compels us, because we are convinced that one died for all" (2 Corinthians 5:14). What does it mean to you to live for Jesus rather than yourself?

3. Think about the people and things that you are most devoted to in life. What would you say drives your devotion to that person or thing?

4. Does the word *devotion* describe how you feel about Jesus? Why or why not?

Pray | Close this study by thanking the Lord for what he has done for you—for his forgiveness, love, grace, and mercy. Confess that you are often devoted to other people and others things before him. Ask him to help you put him first in all areas of your life.

Leader's Guide

Thank you for your willingness to lead your group through this study! What you have chosen to do is valuable and will make a great difference in the lives of others. *The God Who Sees* is a six-session Bible study built around video content and small-group interaction. As the group leader, imagine yourself as the host of a party. Your job is to take care of your guests by managing the details so that when your guests arrive, they can focus on one another and on the interaction around the topic for that session.

Your role as the group leader is not to answer all the questions or reteach the content—the video, book, and study guide will do most of that work. Your job is to guide the experience and cultivate your small group into a connected and engaged community. This will make it a place for members to process, question, and reflect—not necessarily receive more instruction.

There are several elements in this leader's guide that will help you as you structure your study and reflection time, so be sure to follow along and take advantage of each one.

Before You Begin

Before your first meeting, make sure the group members have a copy of this study guide. Alternatively, you can hand out the study guides at your first meeting and give the members some time to look over the material and ask any preliminary questions. Also make sure they are aware that they have access to the streaming videos at any time by following the instructions provided. During your first meeting, ask the members to provide their name, phone number, and email address so you can keep in touch with them.

Generally, the ideal size for a group is eight to ten people, which will ensure that everyone has enough time to participate in discussions. If you have more people, you might want to break up the main group into smaller subgroups. Encourage those who show up at the first meeting to commit to attending the duration of the study, as this will help the group members get to know one another, create stability for the group, and help you know how to best prepare to lead them through the material.

Each of the sessions begins with an opening reflection in the "Welcome" section. The questions that follow in the "Connect" section serve as an icebreaker to get the group members thinking about the topic. Some people may want to tell a long story in response to one of these questions, but the goal is to keep the answers brief. Ideally, you want everyone in the group to get a chance to answer, so try to keep the responses to a minute or less. If you have talkative group members, say up front that everyone needs to limit their answer to one minute.

Give the group members a chance to answer, but also tell them to feel free to pass if they wish. With the rest of the study, it's generally not a good idea to have everyone answer every question—a free-flowing discussion is more desirable. But with the opening icebreaker questions, you can go around the circle. Encourage shy people to share, but don't force them.

At your first meeting, let the group members know each session contains a personal study section they can use to continue to engage with the content until the next meeting. While this is optional, it will help them cement the concepts presented during the group study time and help them better understand the character, nature, and attributes of the God Who Sees. Let them know that if they choose to do so, they can watch the video for the next session by accessing the streaming code. Invite them to bring any questions and insights to your next meeting, especially if they had a breakthrough moment or didn't understand something.

Preparation for Each Session

As the leader, there are a few things you should do to prepare for each meeting:

- **Read through the session.** This will help you become more familiar with the content and know how to structure the discussion times.

- **Decide how the videos will be used.** Determine whether you want the members to watch the videos ahead of time (again, via the streaming access code provided with this guide) or together as a group.

- **Decide which questions you want to discuss.** Based on the length of your group discussions, you may not be able to get through all the questions. So look over the recommendations for the suggested and additional questions in each session and choose which ones you definitely want to cover.

- **Be familiar with the questions you want to discuss.** When the group meets, you'll be watching the clock, so make sure you are familiar with the questions that you have selected. In this way, you will ensure that you have the material more deeply in your mind than your group members.

- **Pray for your group.** Pray for your group members and ask God to lead them as they study his Word.

In many cases, there will be no one "right" answer to the question. Answers will vary, especially when the group members are being asked to share their personal experiences.

Structuring the Discussion Time

You will need to determine with your group how long you want to meet so you can plan your time accordingly. Suggested times for each section have been provided in this study guide, and if you adhere to these times, your group will meet for ninety minutes, as noted below. If you want to meet for two hours, follow the times given in the right-hand column:

Section	90 Minutes	120 Minutes
CONNECT (discuss one or more of the opening questions for the session)	15 minutes	20 minutes
WATCH (watch the teaching material together and take notes)	20 minutes	20 minutes
DISCUSS (discuss the study questions you selected ahead of time)	35 minutes	50 minutes
RESPOND (write down key takeaways)	10 minutes	15 minutes
PRAY (pray together and dismiss)	10 minutes	15 minutes

As the group leader, it is up to you to keep track of the time and keep things on schedule. You might want to set a timer for each segment so both you and the group members know when your time is up. Don't be concerned if the group members are quiet or slow to share. People are often quiet when they are pulling together their ideas, and this might be a new experience for them. Just ask a question and let it hang in the air until someone shares. You can then say, "Thank you. What about others? What came to you when you watched that portion of the teaching?"

Group Dynamics

Leading a group through *The God Who Sees* will prove to be highly rewarding both to you and your group members. But you still may encounter challenges along the way! Discussions can get off track. Group members may not be sensitive to the needs and ideas of others. Some might worry they will be expected to talk about matters that make them feel awkward. Others may express comments that result in disagreements. To help ease this strain on you and the group, consider the following ground rules:

- When someone raises a question or comment that is off the main topic, suggest that you deal with it another time, or, if you feel led to go in that direction, let the group know you will be spending some time discussing it.

- If someone asks a question that you don't know how to answer, admit it and move on. At your discretion, feel free to invite group members to comment on questions that call for personal experience.

- If you find one or two people are dominating the discussion time, direct a few questions to others in the group. Outside the main group time, ask the more dominating members to help you draw out the quieter ones. Work to make them a part of the solution instead of part of the problem.

- When a disagreement occurs, encourage the group members to process the matter in love. Encourage those on opposite sides to restate what they heard the other side say about the matter, and then invite each side to evaluate if that perception is accurate. Lead the group in examining other scriptures related to the topic and look for common ground.

When any of these issues arise, encourage your group members to follow these words from Scripture: "Love one another" (John 13:34), "If it is possible, as far as it depends on you, live at peace with everyone" (Romans 12:18), and "Be quick to listen, slow to speak and slow to become angry" (James 1:19). This will make your group time more rewarding and beneficial for everyone who attends.

Thank you again for taking the time to lead your group. You are making a difference in your group members' lives and having an impact on their journey toward a better understanding of the God Who Sees.

Endnotes

1. Roderick Nash, *Wilderness and the American Mind* (New Haven, CT: Yale University Press, 1982), 425.

2. Sarah Mann, "Deserts in Israel," BeinHarim Tourism Services, October 18, 2021, https://www.beinharimtours.com/deserts-in-israel/.

3. Kayla Muchnik, "Desert in Israel in the Bible and Visiting Them Today," FIRM, October 26, 2022, https://firmisrael.org/learn/deserts-in-israel-in-the-bible-and-visiting-them-today/#:~:text=The%20land%20of%20Israel%20has,Z-in%2C%20Judean%2C%20and%20Araba.

4. "Saint Anthony of Egypt," Britannica, https://www.britannica.com/biography/Saint-Anthony-of-Egypt.

5. Sandra Sweeny Silver, "Who Were the Desert Fathers?" Early Church History, https://earlychurchhistory.org/who-were-the-desert-fathers/.

6. "Macarius the Egyptian," Britannica, https://www.britannica.com/biography/Macarius-the-Egyptian.

7. "Arsenius the Great," Wikipedia, https://en.wikipedia.org/wiki/Arsenius_the_Great.

8. Clifford M. Yeary, "God Encounters Us in Desert's Bareness," Diocese of Little Rock, Arkansas, February 15, 2014, https://www.dolr.org/article/god-encounters-us-deserts-bareness.

9. *The IVP New Testament Commentary Series*, made available by InterVarsity Press on Bible Gateway, https://www.biblegateway.com/passage/?search=matthew+4&version=NIV.

10. "Habakkuk 1—The Prophet's Problem," Enduring Word, https://enduringword.com/bible-commentary/habakkuk-1/.

11. Solomon Schechter, Gotthard Deutsch, Emil G. Hirsch, and Hartwig Hirschfeld, "Hagar," Jewish Encyclopedia, https://www.jewishencyclopedia.com/articles/7021-hagar#.

12. Isidore Singer, M. Seligsohn, Richard Gottheil, and Hartwig Hirschfeld, "Ishmael," Jewish Encyclopedia, https://jewishencyclopedia.com/articles/8251-ishmael.

13. Flavius Josephus, *The Antiquities of the Jews*, book 1, chapter 12, paragraphs 3–4, quoted at https://penelope.uchicago.edu/josephus/ant-1.html.

14. John H. Walton, Victor H. Matthews, and Mark W. Chavalas, *The IVP Bible Background Commentary: Old Testament* (Downers Grove, IL: InterVarsity Press, 2000), 48.

15. Katey Zeh, "When God Tells a Woman to Return to Her Abuser," *Sojourners*, October 22, 2015, https://sojo.net/articles/troubling-texts-domestic-violence-bible/when-god-tells-woman-return-her-abuser.

16. "Genesis 30," *John Gill's Exposition of the Bible,* provided by Bible Study Tools, https://www.biblestudytools.com/commentaries/gills-exposition-of-the-bible/genesis-30/.

17. J. I. Packer, Merrill C. Tenney, and William White Jr., *The Land of the Bible* (Nashville, TN: Thomas Nelson, 1985), 50.

18. Packer, Tenney, and White, *The Land of the Bible*, 50–51.

19. Geoffrey W. Bromiley, general editor, *The International Standard Bible Encyclopedia*, volume III (Grand Rapids, MI: Wm. B. Eerdmans Publishing Company, 1986), 395.

20. "Moab," Wikipedia, https://en.wikipedia.org/wiki/Moab#Religion.

21. George M. Schwab, "Ruth," *The Expositor's Bible Commentary*, volume 2 (Grand Rapids, MR: Zondervan, 2012), 1321.

22. "Gleaning," commentary on Leviticus 19:9–10, Theology of Work, https://www.theologyofwork.org/old-testament/leviticus-and-work/holiness-leviticus-1727/gleaning-leviticus-19910/.

23. "God Calls People to Provide Opportunities for the Poor to Work Productively," commentary on Ruth 2:17–23, Theology of Work, https://www.theologyofwork.org/old-testament/ruth-and-work/god-calls-people-to-provide-opportunities-for-the-poor-and-vulnerable-to-wo/.

24. "What Is the Meaning of the Hebrew Word *Hesed?*," Got Questions, https://www.gotquestions.org/meaning-of-hesed.html.

25. "A Story of *Hesed*," Ligonier, March 22, 2019, https://www.ligonier.org/learn/devotionals/story-of-hesed.

26. Sylvia Schroeder, "What Is *Hesed* and What Does It Tell Us About God's Love for Us?," Christianity.com, June 14, 2021, https://www.christianity.com/wiki/christian-terms/what-is-hesed-love-and-what-does-it-tell-us-about-gods-love-for-us.html.

27. Edwin A. Blum and Jeremy Royal Howard, eds., *Holman Christian Standard Study Bible* (Nashville, TN: Holman Bible Publishers, 2010), 436.

28. "Gates and Doors," Encyclopedia.com, https://www.encyclopedia.com/history/news-wires-white-papers-and-books/gates-and-doors https://www.history.com/topics/ancient-middle-east/mesopotamia.

29. "Sodom and Gomorrah," Britannica, https://www.britannica.com/place/Sodom-and-Gomorrah.

30. "Gates and Doors," Encyclopedia.com, https://www.encyclopedia.com/history/news-wires-white-papers-and-books/gates-and-doors https://www.history.com/topics/ancient-middle-east/mesopotamia.

31. Daniel A. Frese, "The City Gate in Ancient Israel and Her Neighbors," BRILL, https://brill.com/display/book/9789004416673/BP000001.xml?language=en.

32. "Shoe," Britannica, https://www.britannica.com/topic/shoe.

33. Lorne Rozovsky, "Jews and Shoes," Chabad.org, https://www.chabad.org/library/article_cdo/aid/407510/jewish/Jews-and-Shoes.htm.

34. Blum and Howard, *Holman Christian Standard Study Bible,* 436.

35. Blum and Howard, *Holman Christian Standard Study Bible,* 2179.

36. "Bethlehem," Bible Study Tools, https://www.biblestudytools.com/lexicons/greek/nas/bethleem.html.

37. Packer, Tenney, and White, *The Land of the Bible,* 80–81.

38. Fred H. Wight, "Shepherd Life; the Care of Sheep and Goats," from *Manners and Customs of Bible Lands,* Ancient Hebrew Research Center, https://www.ancient-hebrew.org/manners/shepherd-life-the-care-of-sheep-and-goats.htm.

39. "David's Waterfall, Ein Gedi, Israel," Atlas Obscura, https://www.atlasobscura.com/places/david-waterfall#:~:text=The%20waterfall%20and%20river%20get,after%20David's%20victory%20over%20Goliath.

40. "Hebrew Word Study—Paths of Righteousness," Chaim Ben Torah, https://www.chaimbentorah.com/2021/07/hebrew-word-study-paths-of-righteousness-tsedeq-akel/.

41. Estera Wieja, "The Lord Is My Shepherd: IsraelU Explains Psalm 23," FIRM, January 21, 2021, https://firmisrael.org/learn/the-lord-is-my-shepherd-israelu-explains-psalm-23/.

42. Blum and Howard, *Holman Christian Standard Study Bible*, 892.

43. "The Number Seven," Revelation Logic, https://revelationlogic.com/articles/the-number-seven/.

44. "What Is the Biblical Significance of the Number Seven?" GotQuestions, https://www.gotquestions.org/number-7-seven.html.

45. Jill Foley Turner, "Four Lessons from Jesus' Female Funders," National Christian Foundation, March 1, 2023, https://www.ncfgiving.com/stories/4-lessons-from-the-women-who-followed-jesus-from-galilee/.

46. Kathie Lee Gifford and Rabbi Jason Sobel, *The God of the Way* (Nashville, TN: Thomas Nelson, 2022), 162.

47. Gifford and Sobel, *God of the Way,* 162.

48. Craig S. Keener, *The IVP Bible Background Commentary: New Testament* (Downers Grove, IL: InterVarsity Press, 1993), 201–210.

49. Thomas Aquinas, "John 20: Lecture I," Isidore, https://isidore.co/aquinas/english/John20.htm.

50. Gail Wallace, "Mary Magdalene: Five Things You Should Know," The Junia Project, November 21, 2014, https://juniaproject.com/mary-magdalene-5-things-should-know/.

ALSO AVAILABLE

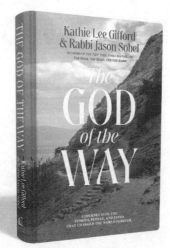

The God the Way
ISBN 9780785290438
On sale September 2022

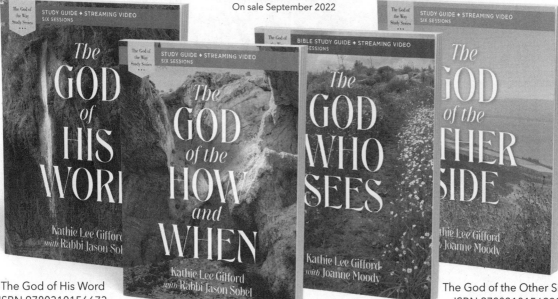

The God of His Word
ISBN 9780310156673
On sale April 2023

The God of the How and When
ISBN 9780310156543
On sale November 2022

The God Who Sees
ISBN 9780310156802
On sale October 2023

The God of the Other Side
ISBN 9780310156932
On sale January 2024

Available wherever books are sold

W Publishing Group

HarperChristian Resources

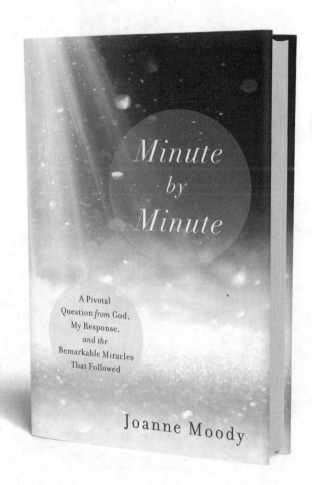

Video Study for Your
Church or Small Group

In this six-session study, Kathie Lee Gifford helps you apply the principles in *The Rock, the Road, and the Rabbi* to your life. The study guide includes video notes, group discussion questions, and personal study and reflection materials for in-between sessions.

Study Guide
9780310095019

DVD
9780310095033

Available now at your favorite bookstore,
or streaming video on StudyGateway.com.

HarperChristian
Resources